Y0-CLG-402

FORWARD MISSION STUDY COURSES

EDITED UNDER THE DIRECTION OF
THE YOUNG PEOPLE'S MISSIONARY MOVEMENT
OF THE UNITED STATES AND CANADA

KOREA IN TRANSITION

N. B.—Special helps and denominational mission study literature for this course can be obtained by corresponding with the Secretary of your mission board or society.

Korea in Transition

By

JAMES S. GALE

Twenty Years a Missionary in Korea

NEW YORK: EATON & MAINS
CINCINNATI: JENNINGS & GRAHAM

C. 1.

TO THE
YOUNG HEARTS OF AMERICA
IN BEHALF OF
THE OLD WORLD OF THE EAST

CONTENTS

APPENDIXES

ILLUSTRATIONS

EDITORIAL STATEMENT

According to the rules of the Young People's Missionary Movement, the Editorial Committee has liberty to make any alterations that it may consider necessary in the manuscripts submitted to it for publication. In making such changes it is customary to consult with the author. The absence of Dr. Gale in Korea has made it impossible to secure from his pen a few additions that were found desirable. These have been made exclusively in Chapters VII and VIII, and have been taken mainly from the reports of other missionaries. These are indicated by quotation marks. There have also been some rearrangement of material and a few elisions. The Committee regrets earnestly that it has been impossible to submit all these changes to Dr. Gale for his approval.

PREFACE

Korea has suddenly emerged from the unknown into the widely advertised of to-day. Politically she is nil, but in the missionary circle she is a first-rate power. Her changes that have taken place externally and internally during the last quarter of a century make one of the startling pages in history. She was nothing, and yet she set in motion the most colossal war-campaign of modern times. She was the Hermit till she was hitched to the longest railway system of the world. But one idea possesses her leaders now, not one of politics, nor one of war, nor one of railway extension, but one of evangelization, to win Asia for Christ, to sound the call to all these dusky multitudes, to tell them of Marconi messages from God, to say peace and good cheer to the downtrodden millions of Asia. This is a large idea for so small a people, but it is good. Shall we not be interested in it too?

JAMES S. GALE.

Seoul, Korea.

THE LAND AND THE PEOPLE

As one first approaches Korea, especially if one has come from the fertile and verdant terraced hills of Japan, the bleakness and barrenness of Korea's mountains is oppressive. Tradition has it that the Korean, in his desire to maintain his independence, deemed that he could do it best by a determined exclusion of all outsiders, and, with the intention of making Korea appear desolate and unattractive, he purposely devastated the whole coast. Whether there is truth in this or not, it remains a fact that the seaward coast of almost all its islands, even where they have a southern exposure, is barren, rugged, and desolate, while ofttimes the northern but landward side is well cultivated, woody, and fertile, and that, while the whole coast-line appears so bleak and bare, when one travels in the interior, one is charmed with the many fertile hills and valleys, teeming with grain and yielding such crops that, while not all of the arable land is cultivated, there is ample for Korea's millions, leaving a large balance in all good years for export.

—Horace G. Underwood

Her resources are undeveloped, not exhausted. Her capacities for successful agriculture are scarcely exploited. Her climate is superb, her rainfall abundant, and her soil productive. Her hills and valleys contain coal, iron, copper, lead, and gold. The fisheries along her coast-line of 1,740 miles might be a source of untold wealth. She is inhabited by a hardy and hospitable race, and she has no beggar class.

—Isabella Bird Bishop

The climate of Korea may be briefly described as the same as that of the eastern part of the United States between Maine and South Carolina, with this one difference, that the prevailing southeast summer wind in Korea brings the moisture from the warm ocean current that strikes Japan from the south, and precipitates it over almost the whole of Korea; so that there is a distinct "rainy season" during most of the months of July and August. This rainy season also has played an important part in determining Korean history.

—Homer B. Hulbert

I

THE LAND AND THE PEOPLE

Korea lies in the same latitude as Boston, New York, Philadelphia, Baltimore, and Washington, 35 to 43 degrees north latitude. Its location is on the eastern rim of Asia, looking southward. At its back is Manchuria, the barbarian land; on its right, China the supreme; on its left, Japan, once the island savage; round about it, many waters; to the east, the Sea of Japan where Russia's fleets still lie submerged; to the west, the Yellow Sea, touching Port Arthur, Dalni, Wei-hai-wei, Chemulpo, and Tsing-tao; to the south, the China Sea with its typhoons and water "dragons."[1]

A journey straight south from Korea would carry you past the east side of the Philippines, between New Guinea and the Celebes, and through west central Australia. North, would take you over Siberia through the mouth of the Lena into the Arctic Ocean. Going due

---

[1] Waterspouts have been "sea-dragons" to the Koreans since time immemorial.

west, you would see Peking, Kabul, Teheran, Constantinople, Rome, New York, and San Francisco. An elevator shaft sunk right through the Northern Hemisphere, would come out in the Atlantic Ocean, distant one hour of sun time from New York.

The Name Korea

Korea is a foreign name, learned a hundred years ago from China, and belonging to a defunct dynasty that fell in 1391 A. D. Like the star that came into collision and was knocked out of being five hundred years ago, whose light still shines, so we still say "Korea." The average native, however, asks: " 'Korea?' What is that? Whom do you refer to?" Korea has had many names. When missionary work first began, it was called "Chosun"; now after unimagined changes it is *Han Guk* or Han, "The Church of Han", "the men of Han", "the golden opportunity in the land of Han", and similar expressions.

Size

Roughly speaking Korea is 600 miles from north to south, and 135 miles from east to west, with an area of about 80,000 square miles. It is about half the size of Japan, one third that of the Province of Ontario, twice that of the state of Kentucky, and about equal in extent to Kansas.

Korea is divided into thirteen provinces. Divisions
Thirteen is an unlucky number, and since this
division was made some ten years ago nothing but a succession of misfortunes has followed. Still, thirteen is associated with our
Lord and his disciples, and while for a time
it may seem to spell defeat and disaster, in the
last great innings thirteen will rise triumphant,
and Korea, we trust, will be joined to this
number forever and forever.

Last year the Financial Adviser's Office is- Population
sued a note concerning the population, number
of houses, and like items, based on police reports and inspection. According to these
returns the province of Kyung kui has a population of 869,000, a half of whom are in and
about the city of Seoul. The most densely
peopled district is south Kyung sang, with a
population of 1,270,214, almost equal to that
of Maryland. The total of these returns, however, shows a population under ten millions.
The Japan Year Book for 1907 considers this
figure too small, and suggests 14,000,000 as
nearer the mark.

Religion ought to insure correctness in a   Native Use of
person's mathematics, but it will take a genera-   Large Numbers
tion or two to trim off the East and bring it

to anything like exactitude in dealing with figures. *Chun-man* or its equivalent is one of the common words, "ten thousand times a thousand". When eight hundred people meet together, thousands are gathered; and fifteen means several score. My old friend Kim prays, "God bless our twenty millions of a family."

"But, Brother Kim, we are not sure that there are twenty millions. Fifteen would seem to be a wide estimate, the census returns show even less."

"Census returns!" echoes Kim, "Dear me, as if we did not know our own family! *I chun man tong po* (20,000,000, brothers and sisters). Everybody says so."

Mountains

Korea has a backbone of mountains, that runs irregularly all down the map. From the Tumen, over against Vladivostok, it drops southwest to Wonsan, then southeast to the Kyung sang border, and from there south along the east border of Chung chong and Chulla. These ridges are not snowcapped nor tall, an elevation of 2,500 feet being a king among them. From the parent range, hills have sprung up everywhere. *"San way yu san, san pul chin"* ("Over the mountains, mountains still, mountains without number"). These hills have talked to the people for hundreds of years, not with so much music as those of Switzerland, nor awakening so patriotic a response, but they have talked with many persuasive voices. Like David, the Korean too, at times, sees his hills skip and dance, and again they weep with him in sackcloth and ashes. So much is said of mountains in Korea that I mention them particularly. They live; in old days their spirits walked about and had their being. They were guardians of the living and watchers over the dead.

There are ten rivers in Korea, but, with **Rivers** the exception of the Tumen, none on the east coast. The hills there come up so close to the seashore that only rivulets are possible. The four noted rivers are the Nak Tong, in the south; the Han, in the center; the Ta Tong, past Ping yang; and the Yalu, in the north.

The soils of Korea are varied, from stiff **Soil** clay to black loam; but the characteristic soil is rotten granite, a white, gritty, porous, barren-looking earth, in which nothing would seem to grow. If you dig it, and inhale the exhalations, you will develop ague till your teeth chatter, your bed rattles, and your whole being vibrates. If you walk on it, it will grind down the soles of your walking shoes in a very short time. Seven hundred miles, with rotten granite here and there, once completely used up two pairs of shoes. This soil is like the soul of the Oriental, it gives little promise of any seed taking root, but once get the roots fastened, then everything grows and flourishes luxuriantly.

Grains

No grain in the Western world stands out preeminently over all others as does rice. Wheat and corn have to do with huge monopolies, and are kings in finance, but rice is the imperial majesty of the cereal world. It is the prettiest grain grown. More people eat rice and flourish on it than on any other grain. Korea is a land of rice. There are beans, and lentils, and barley, and millet, and sesamum, and what not, but these are unseen and unmentioned in the glory of rice. In years when rains are favorable, waving paddy-fields speak the praises of the land all the way from Fusan to the Yalu and the Tumen.

Fruits

Fruits grow well in Korea, coarse pears, hard peaches, wild apples, tasteless dates. But every fruit failure is atoned for in the glorious autumn of persimmons. "Korean persimmons

PLOWING

SAWING TIMBER

are the finest fruit in the world," would be the verdict of many who have had the widest experience and the longest time to judge.

Where every man, woman, and child smokes, shall we not mention tobacco? It too is a mighty king, although it was not known till 1645, being brought in at that time by Prince Chang-yu, who went as ambassador to the first Manchu emperor. I quote from an Eastern writer, Esson Third: "I once heard the Hon. W. W. Rockhill, American minister at Peking, say that Koreans were the greatest smokers in the world. If measured by the time the pipe is in the mouth, they certainly are, but if it be a question of tobacco consumed, the Korean may very easily fall behind the Westerner. He is a deliberate, comfortable, unconscious smoker, so apathetic in his enjoyment of the long pipe, that you hardly know whether he has the smoke or the smoke has him. Cares and anxieties are whiffed away; the fumes curl through his soul softly, benignly, sleepily. The Westerner, on the other hand, pulls fiercely, chews the end, swallows the fumes, and takes the consequences, the result being, that in one half hour he has consumed more tobacco than the Korean will

Tobacco

in a day. To even matters however, Korean
smoking means a united pull, men, women,
and children at it from first cockcrow of the
morning till the curfew says 'Lights out.' It
is as difficult to find a man who does not smoke
as it is to find a ten-year-old son of a gentleman who is not married." This extended reference to tobacco is by no means out of proportion to the place it occupies in the life and
habits of the nation. I notice that among
Korean Church leaders and teachers there is
a quiet but most emphatic putting away of the
pipe and all that goes with it. It is one of the
old kings whose power to command allegiance
is gone forever.

Minerals

Korea is a land supposedly rich in minerals,
such as gold, silver, copper, iron, coal, and
graphite, but because of the sacred character
of the hills, and of the spirits supposed to reside within them, very little mining has been
ventured upon. Now however the audacious
Westerner, who regards neither hill-gods nor
devils, is at it in various parts of the land,
blasting the rocks, sinking shafts deep into
the earth, hauling out the debris, grinding it
to powder, extracting the gold by a magic
spell hitherto undreamed of. Koreans are as-

sociated with him in this work; they see and take part in their humble way, and have won the name of the best miners in the world from managers who have had experience in California, Australia, and elsewhere. One of Korea's future sources of great wealth is undoubtedly mining, but seeing that it is managed and owned by Americans, English, and Japanese, the Korean will come in for only a modest and secondary share of the profits.

Money is called *ton,* and while Chinese tones **Money** are absent from our problem of the language, the problem of ton is always here. Two words wedded together are wafted on every breeze that blows, ton, money, and *pap,* rice. They are the ultimate to which all hearts aspire and all energies seem directed. Twenty years ago Korean money was the cash piece with a hole through it. It took six horses to carry one hundred dollars, and pocket-money was out of the question. While the old cash is still seen in some remote corners of the land, it has almost entirely vanished into the forgotten past, its place taken by the nickel, that has been counterfeited and forged and smuggled and made such unlawful use of that its name and character are ruined forever. Money without the hole in the middle Koreans call *mang-jun* (blind money), and so they naturally inquire, "Will a country not go to pieces that uses blind money?" We still use the nickel to a limited degree, but Japanese currency and a new coinage have come into general use—gold, silver, paper.

Transportation   In America transportation has been from the first by means of carts and wagons, and later by railway, but in Korea it has been and still nearly altogether is by pack-bullock, pony, and coolie. Animals and men are built to carry great loads. Every beast of burden is keyed up like the Brooklyn Bridge to measure its strength by the middle of its back. The coolie, again, differs from the strong man of the West in that his arms are of very little account, little better than a sea-lion's flippers, but when it comes to muscles up and down his back, he is a marvel of strength and can lift 500 pounds. On these patient bodies are slowly carried over the land, rice, beans, hides, timber, fish, salt, Bibles, hymn-books, evangelistic literature, and other burdens, cutting deeper and deeper into the rock and rotten granite the footmarks of successive generations.

The weather in Korea is blocked out in great   **Weather**
lots, not distributed evenly and piece by piece
as at home. When the sun shines it shines for
days with unclouded sky, one month, two
months, three months, with scarce a fleck on
the horizon. Toward the close of these long
spells, the very earth seems to cry out of its
thirsty soul for water. Then the rains come;
first what is called the little *chang-ma* (great
rain), and then the great "great rain." When
this is fully under way, it comes down in
double spouts, tin cans, and buckets. Percival
Lowell says: "During the month of July the
sun rarely shines; it is cloudy almost contin-
ually and nearly every day it rains. It stops
raining only to gather force to rain again, and
the clouds remain the while to signify the rain's
intention to return."   Dr. Underwood says:
"The largest rainfall that is recorded is 5
inches in twenty-four hours; 21.86 inches for
a rainy season. The average yearly rainfall is
36 inches."[1]

Mortals are supposed to have, directly and   **Trolley-cars**
indirectly, an influence on the weather. When   **Blamed for**
the electric trolley-cars were first set running   **Drought**
in Seoul, a peculiar result manifested itself in

[1] *The Call of Korea*, 26.

the life of the nation. We quote from an account that appeared in the *Outlook,* February, 1902. "Little by little the heavens grew dry and the earth rolled up clouds of dust; day followed day with no signs of rain, and the caking paddy-fields grinned and gaped. What could be the cause of it? The geomancers and ground-prophets were consulted, and their answer was, 'The devil that runs the thunder and lightning wagon has caused the drought.' Eyes no longer looked with curiosity but glared at the trolley-cars, and men swore under their breath and cursed the 'vile beast' as it went humming by, till, worked up beyond endurance, there was a crash and an explosion, one car had been rolled over, and another was set on fire, while a mob of thousands took possession of the streets foaming and stamping like wild beasts." This was all on account of the malign influence which these American electric cars were supposed to have on the rainfall of Korea!

Temperature   As for the weather and temperature in general, taking Seoul as our representative point, it is cold in winter and hot in summer. Frequently the temperature falls to zero and even lower, while in summer with a damp, muggy atmosphere, it goes up to 86 or 90 degrees. This constitutes a kind of Turkish bath very trying to the Westerner.

Diseases

To hear a missionary physician read his annual report, and line off the list of diseases that have afflicted Korea's unhappy people for the space of one year, would leave one to infer that the only missing complaint was 'housemaid's knee', for surely everything else in the catalogue from leprosy to anthrax is present; but this is only nominally so. Actually and really we see only a few diseases at work. First and foremost is *hak-jil*, ague. Rare indeed is the person who has not had a periodic chill; as rare as the man who does not smoke, or the man who cannot sleep comfortably on a hot floor with a wooden block behind his ear. Korea is a land of chills and fever. There is also smallpox, but the percentage of pitted faces has decreased wonderfully since the coming in of Jenner's great preventive. Typhus fever is heard of on all sides at certain seasons of the year; and, following close on the summer, comes Asiatic cholera. Consumption is common to all the land, but diseases like typhoid fever and appendicitis seem rare. Scattered cases of leprosy are met with, and, as in Judea in old days, there are always the lame and the halt and the blind.

National Odors   As each nation has its peculiar cut of dress, so each has its national odors apart from race odor. Esson Third says: "The Korean gentleman carries about with him two odors that are specially noticeable to a newcomer. I once made a journey with a Western friend who had a somewhat highly keyed sense of smell, and I remember his stopping short on the road as we walked along, tapping me on the arm and with a long sniff saying:

'There it is again.'

'What is it?' I asked.

'That peculiar smell,' said he.

I sniffed long and hard but there was nothing but the fresh morning breeze, and the delightful odors of hill and field.

'I've smelt it before,' said he, 'and I'll tell you later when I smell it again.'

He tracked that odor for two days, and then we discovered that it came from the black lacquer hat. The odor of lacquer is one of Korea's national smells. The second smell is due to a mixture of garlic, onions, cabbage, salt, fish, and other ingredients, that make up the Korean pickle so greatly enjoyed with their rice. This odor clings like that of Limburger cheese, and follows the native to church and into all the other walks of life."

Compared with the Western world, with its **National Sounds** indescribable hubbub, Korea is a land of the most reposeful silence. There are no harsh pavements over which horses are tugging their lives out, no jostling of carts or dray-wagons, no hateful clamor that forbids quiet conversation, but a repose that is inherent and eternally restful. The rattle of the ironing-sticks is not nerve-racking, but rather serves as a soporific to put all the world to sleep. Apart from this, one hears nothing but the few calls and echoes of human voices. What a delightfully quiet land is Korea! In the very heart of its great city Seoul, you might experiment at midday in the latest methods of rest-cure and have all the world to help you.

Among other restful national features are the **The Roads** roadways. They are not surveyed at right angles and fenced in with barbed-wire, but are left to go where they please, do as they like, and take care of themselves, just as suits them. Hence a Korean road will find the easiest possible way over a hill. It will narrow itself down to a few inches rather than pick a quarrel

with a rock or hummock on the way, or again
to please you it will widen out like a Western
turnpike.   To follow a Korean road is like
reading one of Barrie's novels, you meet with
surprises and delights all along the way.

General Aspect

While the general aspect of Korea is a sad
and desolate one, that of a mountainous land
shorn bare of its trees and foliage, there are
pretty vistas and views that break out occasionally from behind the hills. As a people Koreans
thoroughly enjoy natural beauty, but they have
taken no steps whatever to conserve it.   Trees
and grass and brushwood and flowering shrubs.
everything in fact that grows, comes under the
woodman's sickle, and is shaved bare as the
locks of a Buddhist priestess.   Around the capital, especially, the hills have been denuded so
often that the rains have washed away the
upper soil and left them gray-topped and bare.
There is a wide field for the work of forestry in
Korea.

Houses

In the hidden and often picturesque nooks
nestle clusters of brown huts thatched with
straw. In and out of these mud beehives go
people dressed in immaculate white. A hut
is built by first pounding the earth for the
foundation-stones, then setting up the posts

BUILDING A HOUSE

BEATING TURNIP SEED INTO MEAL

and beams. Between the posts are put cross-bars and bamboo lathing, then mud is plastered on the inside and out. It is not just common mud, but carefully prepared mud, that will not crack and let in the wind. For flooring, flat stones are used, placed over flues; a thin layer of mud covers the surface and makes it even. Then the whole inside is papered with white paper on the walls and thick yellow oil-paper on the floor. The windows are of paper also. When the fire is built in the kitchen, the heated vapors from it pass underneath the living-rooms; the stone floors warm gently, and here, cross-legged, you take up your abode.

A friend called just now, and I asked him **Dress** to please take off his horsehair hat and let me weigh it. The whole hat, crown, brim, border, string, and other parts, weighed just one and a quarter ounces. How light and ethereal the Korean garb is, especially in summer! If we follow Mr. Kim from the crown of his head to the tip of his toe, his wearing-apparel would run thus: first, the ounce and a quarter hat; then the inner cap, lighter still; then the headband, equally light; then the spectacles, the long outer robe, the inner coat, the rattan jacket, worn in hot weather next the skin, the

pantaloons, the leggings, the socks, the shoes.
The material is cotton goods made wide and
loose and roomy. In a dress like that you may
sit all day cross-legged without a suggestion
of bagging at the knees, perhaps because they
are all bags, and wide enough to accommodate
the wearer two or three times over. White is
the prevailing color, but bright tints and hues
are interspersed, especially with young people,
so that a school yard alive at recreation hour
looks like a fluttering congregation of blue-
birds, orioles, and robins. The belt, or girdle-
string, binds the man of the East together, just
as suspenders serve for girders and mainstays
for the man at home. The woman's dress differs somewhat from that of the man, but white,
loose, baggy, badly gripped and held in place,
unsuited for a busy, dirty world such as this is,
would apply equally to both.

Food

The Korean is a stranger to sweets, and
no sugar-sticks ever tempted the children of
his land. Honey is used in small quantities,
but chocolate creams, and fudge, and sweet
sodas through a straw, and ices, he never
dreamed of even in connection with Nirvana.
In place of these his delights have been of the
salt and peppery kind. He has chilli sauce and

chilli soy, salt and red peppers mixed in pickle, and greens and soup. The average foreigner who tries Korean food is compelled at short intervals, to open his mouth, draw in cool breaths, and fan wildly. The tears in his eyes and his general look of agony would lead one to infer that he had been dining off live coals instead of plain rice and cabbage pickle, and soup and beans and soy. This is the Korean average meal every day and all the year round. They are not great meat eaters, rice, beans, and cabbage taking the place of meat, potatoes, and bread. It is a very monotonous fare, and yet men are strong in the strength of it and can work like horses and carry enormous loads.

In soul the Korean is the son of a Chinaman, but in language he is related to Japan. He can sound both *l* and *r,* while the Japanese has to say *gay-roo* for girl, and the Chinaman says *Amellican* for American. The Korean stands between them not in heart and geographical position only, but in a still greater sense, we trust, that will be manifest in days to come. Korean is a simple speech, unartificialized by a fixed set of rules and a printed literature like our own. It belongs to Gospel times, for while it labors hard to express Romans and Gala-

Language

tians, the Gospels speak forth from it beautifully. While expressing the simplicities of
life most appropriately, it is a hard language
to learn with its honorifics and Chinese de-
rivatives.

The Complete but Changing Picture

Will the reader then please enter into this introductory picture of Korea, joining companionship with these millions dressed in their odd
garments, moving about in cities, among the
mountains, and between the waving rice-fields,
blessed with the sunshine and the rain, sorrow-
ing, suffering, ignorant of time, ignorant of
eternity, dying off one generation after another, each smoking its pipe of self-satisfaction,
dreaming that it was rich and increased in
goods and had need of nothing, speaking no
end of salutation, peace, peace, when there was
no peace? On this procession has wended,
till twenty years and more ago, when there
struck an hour on the clock that marks off
the ages, and the gates of the Hermit swung
wide open, and in stepped forces that have
since been mingling mightily with what has
been touched on in the opening paragraphs.
All things are changing so rapidly, so radically,
that we wonder whither we are going. To
this quiet, unsophisticated people have come no

end of wild surprise and political upheaval, unutterable despair and blind suicide.

But in the midst of this crashing and break- **Spiritual Voices —Peter** ing up of every ideal come callers not dreamed of before. One is Peter. He says: "Are you a low-caste man? So was I. Are you dead beat? So was I. Do you long for victory? So did I. One name solved all my troubles, just one name, let me whisper it to you, 'Jesus, Jesus, Jesus;' so the vibrations carry it as by wireless telegraphy from Peter's lips to the farthest limits of the land."

Another preacher follows, hard to under- **Paul** stand. Paul is his name. He asks: "Are you an aristocrat and a scholar? God has no use for aristocrats. He wants sinners, the unthankful, the unholy. Which class do you belong to? Stricken from off my exalted seat, down in the dust I first recognized him. Shut your eyes to the world, get into Straight street, and try prayer."

Another preacher is Jesus' mother. Mary **Mary** says: "So many people were round about him I could not get near. All I wanted was just to see Jesus. His answer was: 'Who wants me? My mother? Why all you Korean people need to see me just as badly as my mother does. Look on me as she does with love, and you'll be my mother, and sister, and brother.'"

Korea's heart beats one with China. The chords struck across the Yalu find response here. She is under Japan tighter than lock and key can make her. Has God a purpose for the Far East with his hand upon her, and she between these two mighty questions of the world, China and Japan?

SUGGESTIONS FOR USING THE QUESTIONS

The questions below, as their title indicates, are intended to be *suggestive*. They make no pretense to review the contents of each chapter. Such a memory test can easily be constructed by any leader or student by writing out the contents of the chapter and then expanding them without the aid of the text. The present questions are intended to stimulate original thought, and they therefore use the text-book only as a point of departure.

Leaders may find it profitable to assign some of these questions in advance for study and discussion. It will usually be better to discuss a few questions thoroughly, rather than to try to cover the entire set. In many cases the leader can fit them better to the use of a particular class by careful rewording.

If they are used in private study, it is recommended that conclusions be written out. It is not expected that the average student will be able to answer all these questions satisfactorily; otherwise there would be little left for the class session. Let results, however frag-

mentary, be brought to the class and supplemented
by comparison and discussion.

The questions marked * are perhaps most worth
discussing in detail.

SUGGESTIVE QUESTIONS ON CHAPTER I

AIM: TO COME INTO SYMPATHY WITH THE LAND AND
PEOPLE

I. *Space and Time Distances.*

1. Compare the area and population of Korea
with that of the State or Province in which
you live.

2. How does it contrast in area and population
with the combined States of New York and
Pennsylvania?

3. How large would the States of New York and
Pennsylvania seem to you if we had only the
Korean means of intercommunication?

4. How far do you think you would have traveled
from home under such circumstances?

5. About how long would it take you to go from
Boston to Richmond, Virginia, on a pony, if
the roads were bad?

6.* Try to estimate the relative size of Korea and
the United States measured by the time consumed in travel.

7. Try to imagine what your life would be like
if you were entirely cut off from modern
means of transportation.

II. *Influence of Environment on Character.*

8. What sort of climate would you choose for a
nation in order that its inhabitants might develop the strongest character?

9. Find on a map of North America points which approximate the latitude of the northern and southern limits of Korea.

10. What are the relative advantages of a nation of extended latitude and extended longitude?

11.* Try to discover some of the influences that have made the Koreans inexact in their mental processes.

12. What do the comparative methods of smoking reveal to you of Korean and Western character?

13. What advantages will Korea derive in the future from her comparatively compact area?

14.* What things in the physical features of Korea give you most hope for the future?

III. *The Inevitable Changes.*

15.* If Korea were made over to you as a gift, what measures would you take to improve your property? Name in order of their importance.

16.* Describe what you think would be the effect of each of these physical improvements on the life of the people.

17. To what extent are these changes inevitable in Korea?

18. What would be the probable effect upon an ignorant country boy without principles of being suddenly thrust into city life?

19.* In what ways does this example illustrate the present position of Korea?

20. What would be the effect of Western civilization upon a primitive people without the constraint of Christianity?

21. For what reasons do you think this land deserves the sympathy of the Christian Church?

REFERENCES FOR FURTHER STUDY
CHAPTER I

I. *Resources.*

  Hulbert: The Passing of Korea, ch. I, pp. 274, 275.

  Bishop: Korea and Her Neighbors, pp. 14-18, 391, 392, 445.

  Underwood: The Call of Korea, pp. 23-35.

  Gifford: Every-day Life in Korea, pp. 20-22.

  Noble: Ewa: A Tale of Korea, pp. 11-13.

II. *Transportation.*

  Hulbert: The Passing of Korea, ch. XVIII.

  Bishop: Korea and Her Neighbors, p. 128.

III. *Recent Improvements.*

  Hulbert: The Passing of Korea, ch. XXXIV.

  Bishop: Korea and Her Neighbors, pp. 435-443.

THE NATION'S PRESENT
SITUATION

HISTORICAL SKETCH

It seems best, as Dr. Gale has done, to avoid a discussion of the causes leading to the Japanese control of Korea. On this subject bitter charges and countercharges have been made, and the complete truth is not easy to discover. A brief table is given, however, to indicate the principal political events since 1876:

1876. First foreign treaty of Korea with Japan.

1883. First treaties with the United States, Germany, and Great Britain. First American minister to Korea.

1885. China and Japan sign convention agreeing not to send troops into Korea without previous consultation. Chinese influence dominant.

1894. China sends troops into Korea to repress Tong-hak rebellion. This leads to war between China and Japan. Japanese influence dominant.

1895. Queen of Korea assassinated by Japanese and Koreans.

1896. King takes refuge in Russian legation in Seoul. Russian influence dominant.

1898. Japan and Russia agree to recognize the independence of Korea and to abstain from interference.

1904. Russia's encroachments lead to war with Japan. Korea agrees to accept the advice of Japan as to administration, and Japan guarantees the independence of Korea. Virtual Japanese protectorate.

1905. Japan secures control of the foreign relations of Korea. Marquis Ito becomes Resident-General.

1907. Emperor of Korea forced to abdicate in favor of the Crown Prince. The Resident-General in complete control.

In general it may be said that Japan has assumed control of Korea in order to exclude any further possibility of Russian intrigue, to which the Korean government had always been susceptible. The administration initiated by Marquis Ito is undoubtedly far more efficient and modern than that which it displaced. On the other hand, it is claimed that the Koreans have suffered many abuses at the hands of the Japanese soldiers and settlers.

II

THE NATION'S PRESENT SITUATION

Over the hill from my home, in a little house with tiled roof, lives a widow, Mrs. Shin. Her family consists of mother-in-law, son seventeen years of age, long waited for, now a man, daughter fourteen, and Samuel her youngest, aged four. It did not attract much attention from the outside world, this home, but it was everything to the humble inhabitants thereof. Su-nam, the tall son, was the new, strong flagstaff around which age and tender years rallied. Through many seasons of hardship and sorrow, this home had come to commit its way to God, to trust also in him, knowing that he would bring it to pass. True Christians they were and Su-nam was their hope and joy.

He was on a visit to Ping yang when yesterday (July 27), between the torrents of falling rain, there came a telegram to me saying, "Su-nam drowned." What a dire stroke for that poor home in two short words, a double-edged sword cutting to the hilt through the

Sorrow's Unit of Measure

For introductory material to this chapter see opposite page.

center of the soul! With this information in hand I crossed the hill to Mrs. Shin's house. They were at evening meal in the little veranda round a very small table. With smiles they greeted my coming, for I was their friend, and would bring good cheer and hope. What cruelty! I was to turn all these smiles into an agony of woe unspeakable. "Alas," I said, "I have news, such news as will break your hearts, God help us all!" Every face instantly fixed itself into an expression of pained suspense, and I went on, "God has called Su-nam. He is drowned." The little girl of fourteen, as if shot with a rifle bullet, broke into a cry that would melt the soul; the mother dropped on her face but no word passed her lips; the old grandmother, whose hopes were on this boy, lifted up her heart to heaven and said, "We thank thee, O Father. Thou didst give Su-nam; thou hast taken Su-nam; blessed be thy name."

Korea's Desolation

Multiply this heart-breaking scene to a family of fifteen millions, and make their little table this desolated peninsula, and you will have some idea of what Korea has passed through in the last few sad years. Indescribable is the wailing that has gone up and beating of the breast over the death and burial of hopes, aspirations, and long-cherished desires.

Korea's was a patriarchal form of govern-ment from the beginning. Officials were often still but callow youths, but by reason of office they were magnified and glorified into mature age with beard and rod of authority. The peo-ple at large were their children, whom they fathered, arrested, beat, stood in a corner, kept in after school, or set digging weeds, just as they saw fit, and no reply would be forthcom-ing, except perhaps a wail open-mouthed and loud such as children break out with, but with a voice fifty or sixty years of age.

The Way that Failed

Under this system the people individually were nothing, and they were reasonably con-tent to be so, provided their ancient customs continued. They were oppressed and down-trodden, but it was oppression dealt out accord-ing to custom, and custom is higher than law. This was their country and they were free to love or kill each other with no foreigner to interfere. To them patriotism consisted in minding your own business, and keeping clear of the official's long-handled paddle, but on the opening of the gates and the inrush of Western life all is changed. Now Korea must awake

Misrule

and adjust herself to a new age, or the age
would roll over and crush her forever. For
twenty years Korea had a chance to get into
line with these new forces, but it was not to be.
It was a question of life and death, but she was
not able. Many saw it, many spoke thereof.

**The Retired
Emperor**

As great father for the land was the deposed
emperor, chosen of God to bring his people to
a state of wo unexampled, under which however we believe there lie hidden hopes higher
than she has ever dreamed of. The emperor
could say as Louis XIV did, *"L'état c'est moi"*
("The state, I am the state"), though he forgot
that he was not the twentieth century, and
forgot other outside forces as well. His walk
was backward. Kings of the Orient until recent
years have favored the rearward march in their
movings, or else their eyes have been hopelessly fixed in the back of the head; for with
fixed gaze on *Yo-sun* (2300 B. C.), they have
backed up into all sorts of confusion, never
seeing where they were going until too late,
dreaming only of the past from which they
had emerged, no progress ever contemplated,
no reform undertaken lest it detract from the
glory of *Yo* and *Sun* the king-gods of the
Golden Age. The retired emperor was un-

doubtedly an instrument used of God to humble his own land. It was impossible to bring him into touch with any new era. He was kind and gentle and often full of compassion, but a suggestion of reform would rouse the demon within him, and he would clap thumbscrew and torture rack onto the friend of yesterday and have him drawn and quartered forthwith. During the twenty years that he was on trial for his life, he failed at every point. This is the first thing to remember in considering the position of Korea to-day politically. She was brought to it by the retired emperor being out of touch with the age he lived in.

There was another factor to be reckoned Japan with, namely, Japan; and the retired emperor and his people both emphatically disliked Japan. From earliest times they had marked her by abusive terms *Wa-ro* (slaves of Wa), *To-man* (island savages), *Wai-nom* (foreign knaves); while Japan spoke of Koreans as *Han-kak* (honored guests of Han). Nothing could bring them together. Religion? The Japanese prayed to Buddha and the Shinto gods, while Korea was Confucian. Japan exalted the sword, and Korea despised her, for she herself worshiped the pen.

Korea through its ruler was out of touch
with the age in which it lived; in heart, sympathy, and tradition it was out of touch with
the Japanese, and yet here were these three
gradually coming to occupy the same room,
and the same bed, at the same time: the twentieth century, the Korean emperor, and the
spirit of Japan; unsuited as fire and water, or
wood and lightning, destined to kick and smash
and resist until one of them was reduced to
hopeless and non-resisting silence.

The emperor too and his people were not at
one. Esson Third wrote some years ago: "The
Korean emperor has no confidence in his people, and his people have no use for the Japanese, and the Japanese have no faith in the
emperor. Reverse it and it is still correct. The
emperor mistrusts the Japanese, the Japanese
have no confidence in the people, and the people despise the emperor." Reform was stamped
out. The best and most enlightened men were
shut up in prison. It was a fight on the part of
the old emperor, single-handed, against his own
people, against the onrolling centuries, with
the Japanese accompanying, keeping pace and
persistently shouting "Banzai" (long live our
emperor).

Then it was that men's hearts began to fear Looking Toward Christianity and to turn toward Christianity. Wiser ones said, "All the forces of the universe are bearing down upon us; unless God help we are lost." It was the beginning of the awakening in the Korean's soul to the helpless condition of his country. Once, on a call at his home, Prince Min said to the writer, "Pray for Korea. God can help us if no one else can." Eyes that never looked heavenward before did so now in view of uncertainties.

The emperor, by his old "underground" First Retributive Results methods, was in touch with Russia, anxious for her belated civilization, if he could not hold on to 2000 B. C., but every move turned against him, everything was out of gear. On November 17, 1905, in the dead of night, at the Palace in Chung dong, Seoul, the first payment was made for all the mistaken years, the wrongs done and suffered, and the lies told and unrepented of. It was made by the signing of the treaty of that date, giving over to the Japanese government the control of Korea's foreign affairs. On receipt of this news, Prince Min concluded that his country was gone and that he would die with it. He locked himself away from all his friends, wrote out his will, and a few farewell letters, and then with a dull, short pocket-knife accomplished his own quietus. Written large round his name, Korea will ever read the sentence, "Sweet and seemly is it to die for one's fatherland."

The Final Crisis Again in July, 1907, another crisis was reached. The nation that had so long attempted to sail in a leaky boat, and had persistently clubbed any man who had tried to stop the chinks, was going down. The water was deep and all straws were caught at, Russia, The Hague, Mr. Hulbert, Hawaiian Petition, Bethell and Company, appeal to rifles; but everything failed. The Japan-Korea Treaty of July 24, 1907, resulted, and the last act of the drama was the exit of the old emperor-king. He was asked to move out and make way for oncoming generations, to sign away all rights as emperor, king, autocrat; to abdicate once and for all. The wildest cry was of no avail. There was no resisting; force sufficient was back of the order to project him into eternity, and so he bowed to the inevitable. According to the understanding of the people at large, the last breath was drawn, and Korea had expired.

The Aftermath A mad sort of spurious patriotism started

into being, with suicide, chopping off of fingers, sworn oaths, guerilla warfare, flint-lock resistance. It still goes on to a considerable degree, while the poor people in the valleys, caught between the contending forces, have to pay the price of Korea's past failure. With the question as to how in other ways she came to such a pass as this, as to where the right and wrong of it lay, as to what ought to have been done and what ought not to have been done, it is not in our province to deal. Here she is to-day. If it had not been the Japanese, certainly the twentieth century single-handed would have crushed the old emperor and all he represented out of existence. Evidently the purpose in this plan of God was to bring Korea to a place where she would say, "All is lost, I am undone." Like Mrs. Shin and her household, nothing remained for the people but to commit the whole burden of it to the Lord himself.

First and foremost they had lost their country. There have been men who have had no citizenship, and who have passed the pilgrimage of life without flag or nationality, unprotected by state or consular arm of the law, but most people would feel unhappy under such cir-

Looking for a Country

cumstances. Even Paul emphatically made announcement of the fact that he was a Roman citizen, and as good a man as Dr. Guido F. Verbeck knocked at the state entrance of Japan, requesting that they please take him in, as he and his family were without country and felt shelterless.

John Chinaman's Country in Heaven

Still, there are those who overcome such sentiments and walk the earth victoriously. A Chinese lived in Yokohama some twelve years ago. He was a house-painter by occupation, and went about wearing a very much bedaubed suit of clothes, caked here and there with white and green and yellow. He was a Christian and attended church regularly. When the leader said, "Let any one pray who will," John never failed to take part. The gladness of his soul spoke itself forth in a kind of Cantonned Japanese, the full meaning of which was known to himself and God only. When the *Shinasan* (Mr. Chinaman) prayed, many a face in the room became wreathed in smiles and sometimes a hand was necessary over the mouth to help hold the hearer steady. John paid no attention, he cared not who laughed at his prayers, he was happy, God had forgiven him and though a Chinese, he had said good-by to the world, and cut his cue off. One day a Korean friend met him and said, "Honorable sir from the great country, where is your cue?" "Cue? Cue belong no good, makee cut off." "But you will not dare to go home, you have lost your country." *"Maskee* country," said John, "my country belong *Htien-kuoa, Htien-kuoa"* ("Heaven, Heaven"), pointing upward.

Could we but convey John's upward look and happy spirit to the hearts and homes of Korea, we should have done the work for which all this agony of sweat and blood has prepared the way. The Korean says: "I have no country, no citizenship, no flag, no land that is my own, only the skeleton and remains. They are worse than nothing, ghastly, ought to be buried out of sight," and the hoplessness of a worldly man with none of the world's backing settles over him. He did not know that his country was worth anything till he lost it. He abused it and disgraced it for generations, still it was his; now it is dead, and no man is on hand to raise the dead to life.

Hope for the Hopeless

In former days when the state threatened collapse there were supports available. Russia served at times, then France, sometimes China or England. Says friend Kim:

Human Failure. Divine Faithfulness

"America we were sure of, for the first article in our treaty with her read, 'If other powers deal unjustly with either government, the one will exert its good offices, on being informed of the case, to bring about an amicable arrangement, thus showing its friendly feelings.' England joined the enemy, and even America went back on us. Verbeck may have found a door to knock at but there is no door for lost Han." How like oil on the troubled waters of the soul fall such sentences as these, "My kingdom is not of this world." "Resist not." "For our citizenship is in heaven." There also we have our "city which hath the foundations, whose builder and maker is God."

Like a Fairy Tale

The possibility of a poor Korean, really and truly under such circumstances, knocking at the palace gates of heaven and making application for citizenship in the name of Jesus, being received, his name recorded, and a happy peaceful heart given as proof thereof is like a fairy tale of the Taoists. It is like the story of the resurrected Jesus to Peter and his companions, a something that the women must have hatched up, but that sound-minded men could not receive.

My friend Kim says: "We have no king. The one we had was a poor makeshift, to be sure, but anything is better than no king. He would never take a reprimand. The number of heads of chief officers that dropped during his reign was astounding. He was mighty in having his own way, and in keeping the people under. He used to say: 'Don't make a noise. Don't talk about the government. Don't fight each other and send petitions to the Palace. Just eat your rice, and do your work, and be good.' When the people attempted to carry on the Independence Club, his majesty put up a notice on the Bell-kiosk, 'Let there be no meetings, or shout-talk of any kind in the streets. You are commanded every man to stay at home and mind his own business.' He handcuffed us, he robbed us, he paddled us, he hanged and quartered us, he lived for himself alone and for his worn-out superstitions, but it was better than no king. So deeply is the patriarchal thought written on the heart, that bees could as easily swarm without a queen-bee as Korea lift up its head without some choice in the way of ruler."

Many Faults but Still Their King

The old king, after having been execrated for twenty years or more, suddenly swings

Turning to a Heavenly King

into a niche of honor, by virtue of the death that his kingship dies. The Japanese, through the present cabinet, put his son on the throne in his place, but Kim knows nothing of that. He repeats, "Alas, there is no king to-day." For these kingless, downcast, fifteen millions of Koreans there was written long ago, The name of your King is "Wonderful, Counsellor, Mighty God, Everlasting Father, Prince of Peace."

The Higher Vision

What a day in which to proclaim the nature of his kingdom! He too was an Oriental. He too lived in a land fallen as to kingship. He too felt the shame of the nation's loss. He died with and for guilty men. "He lives and holds in his hand all the kingdoms of the world, Japan as well as Judea. He brought you here under the harrow; he sent the Japanese that you might be taught to yield to him." An old man with teeth out and cheeks fallen in says, "I used to be an officer of state myself, and my heart was caked hard with the doings thereof, but since I came to Jesus and he is my King, I love even the Japanese, and the mountains of the west over which my sun is setting are all lighted up with glory."

Since 1122 B. C., when the Chinese sacred

books were first brought to Korea by Viscount **National Love of Literature**
Ki, Korea has been a worshiper of literature.
As the sycee-silver shoe might represent China,
and the two-handed sword Japan, the brush
pen with the bamboo handle would be the
choice of all for Korea.   Happy the man who
knows its companionship, who can grip it verti-
cally, strike across the page and bring his line
to the required finish, mark it downward and
not weaken at the end, cut east and west, dot,
and turn the corner.   It requires years to
learn all this.   The labor-blunted hand of the
Westerner could never do it.   The joy of writing the characters takes its rise high up in the
Korean's heaven.   Then the reading of them
is like deciphering messages from the gods.
The man who could do so well, was honored
by king and commoner alike.   To encourage
this sublime art, there were periodical examinations held, to which candidates presented themselves from all corners of the land.   Many came
hundreds of miles all the way on foot, in the
hope of gaining some distinction at the *Koaga*
(Examination).   Though you failed, the fact
that you were a candidate was distinction un-
questioned.   To pass and become a *Koup-je*
clothed you with Korea's most excellent glory.

Honor for
Education

Throughout the land were schoolrooms, where lads gathered for study, singing out the lesson all together at the top of the voice. A third of the time they read, a third of the time they wrote, a third of the time they composed. So greatly are literature and education honored, that the common title, Mr. (*So-bang*), means really "Schoolroom" or we might better say "School-man"; so we have "School-man" this and "School-man" that. It may be Pak who digs weeds in the paddy-field and never studied a day in his life, but he too is "School-man" Pak, and he addresses his fellow laborer Koak as "School-man" Koak. Everybody is a "School-man," all over the land, by reason of the desire to share in even the shadow of the glory that goes with literature.

Old Literature
and School
Methods
Forsaken

The inrush of Goths and Vandals in 410 and the sacking of Rome would not be considered by a Korean more terrible than the forces that have recently pushed through the gateways of Korea. Western civilization, the twentieth century, and the Japanese are quite as fearful and barbarous a combination. Before these all the choice idols of the land have fallen, and chief among them was Chinese literature, now gone down to the eternal shades.

There are no more periodic examinations, no more singing off of the classics in hope of high honor and distinction, no more meditating over the *Book of Changes*. The bamboo pen lies dishonored, and the barking of ten-inch guns takes the place of infant voices singing out "Heaven blue, earth yellow," and the other old school phrases.

The Korean is a gentleman by instinct, he worships intellect and not the god of force. In his tears over his fallen divinity, he fumbles at the sword, thinking to try it, but the sword is not his, as it was not Peter's. What shall he do for something that will take the place of all that he has lost? When in tears, just at this time there comes to him the Bible, sixty-six books, oldest in the world, written by thirty-six writers or more, among whom were shepherds and plowmen, as well as kings and princes. It stretches in its range over fifteen hundred years, including history, doctrine, and prophecy, in prose and verse; it points to the past, even back of the days of Yo and Sun; it speaks with kingly authority as to the present; turning its searchlights on into the vistas of the future; it tells of God, what he is, and what he has done; it solves the problem of

Finding Biblical Truth

man, and his lost condition; it leads one on into places of deliverance, victory, and peace. Was there ever such a literature, and was there ever such a time as this? Let all hearts and hands unite in getting into his soul these divine and kingly truths. Some who were never scholars in the ancient classics have become men of mighty influence, because the heart has been filled with the sayings of sages such as Moses, Daniel, Isaiah, Peter, Paul, and John.

Nai-woi

Among the breaking down of ancient customs to-day, *Nai-woi* is destined to go likewise. Now Nai-woi is not an Anamese nor an East Indian god, but an old Korean custom of mature years and long standing. It has been like the feathers and paint on the red Indian giving him glory in the eyes of men, to the obliteration of his female partner, who is buried under the monotonies of life with the papoose on her back. Nai-woi means 'inside-outside', 'prisoner-freeman', 'woman-man'. Because of Nai-woi, Korean women have gradually disappeared from the world of recognition, to the world of slavery and imprisonment.

Woman's
Freedom

History has from time immemorial shown us a locked-up world of women, women made prisoners, bought and sold. Occasionally one has risen superior to her wrist-rings and shackles, and made her name and influence felt, but the woman's world has been the dark curtained region full of oppression and despair. Jesus came and set the women of the world free. He seems to be the only one who knows how to unlock her prison-house, so as not to have it open into another equally woful. Korea's women have been under the closest sort of battened down hatches. But the twentieth century has come in, holding aloft the name of Jesus and proclaiming all women free. What a consternation has been created in the breaking down of the middle wall, Nai-woi, fraught as it is with great danger as well as great hope.

High women of the land who never saw **Her New Perils** sunshine or the open air till a few days ago, are suddenly shoved pell-mell into public functions and asked to drink champagne and be hail-fellow-well-met with all sorts and conditions of men. With no precedent behind, with no knowledge accompanying, and with no mature vision of the future, these women are drifting into uncertainty with all the barbed wires and safeguards of Nai-woi done away.

The East is full of color and can match the
most glaring extremes in a way pleasing and
grateful to the eye, but let it get out of its world
into the tints of the West, and green screams
out against magenta, and purple and red fight
furiously. So in dress, shovel hats and hollow-
chested shirt-waists run riot with black skirts
waisted high up under the arms. How sadly
the once dreamy woman's world of the East
has developed under the harsh sunlight of to-
day!

Where is hope to come from? Only from
Jesus, seems the consensus of opinion, even
among unbelievers. In lowly companionship
with him the Eastern woman may safely meet
the breaking down of custom. A few days
ago a Christian official on a call said: "Our
women are emancipated from the slavery that
besets them, only to fall into a deeper and more
deadly one. May God in his mercy protect
and defend them!"

As I write I see the face of one called To-
hong (Peach-red). She was a low-class dancing-girl, bought and sold. Restoration was a
word not applicable to her, for she never was
right. She was born lapsed and lived lapsed.
Over the walls of the world that encircled her

came the story of Jesus, a man, a wise and pure
man, pure as God is pure, in fact a God as God
is God, yet it was said that he loved lost and
fallen women. Peach-red had never before
heard of such a being. Her soul was sick, and
she wondered if she could but meet him what
he would say to "the likes of her", and if he
really could cure soul-sickness. When or where
or how Peach-red met Jesus I know not; that
she met him I most assuredly know. Seven
years had rolled away, and out of my life
passed the name of Peach-red. It was forgotten in the multitude of names that crowded
on me. One Sunday, after service in a great
meeting-house of some two thousand people,
with this and that one coming forward to say
"Peace," there appeared before me a smiling
face known and yet not known. "Don't you
remember me? Baptized me seven years ago.
My old name was Peach-red." Here was this
woman in value once less than zero, crowned
with the light and liberty and growth in grace
of seven years. On long journeys over the
mountains, hundreds of miles, on such a mission as Paul's through Europe had gone the
unwearied feet of Peach-red. For seven years
it had been a pilgrimage of victory, and she

was here to-day with an overflowing heart to thank the Lord.

Social Barriers Removed

By her side sat Madam Yee, wife of one of Korea's noted men, once imprisoned, curtained round, secluded, shadowed by the awful form of Nai-woi, proud too, not deigning to look at such refuse as Peach-red. To-day they sit together and Madam Yee says: "You know so much of the Bible. Let me listen while you read it. Truly you are dear." Jesus had broken Nai-woi so that Madam Yee came to this crowded meeting-house. He had bridged the chasm that divided these two women. He had delivered the poor dancing-girl from the life of a broken Nai-woi and from the slavery under which she was held. Surely at such a day as this when the woman's world is crashed into and the dividing walls are down, we need the gospel to point out the new and better way.

"Face"

The word "face," *Mo-yang,* flourishes widely in the Far East and has one of the first claims on the heart of Korea. Be the dress however fine, unless the face be comely the man stands at a disadvantage. If he be furrowed and bristled over with a jungle of hair, the wearer may be Thomas Carlyle, and may have written *Sartor Resartus,* but that does

not redeem him from a certain flavor of bar-
barism. Perhaps the face of Yüan Shih-k'ai
would as nearly answer the ideal of Korea as
any other, round, well set, carried with all
dignity, agreeable to look upon, proud, in-
scrutable. This pertains to the outer face,
but there is an inner face that is the real question. We notice it when he says, "If I be put
to shame, so that others know it, I have lost
face." Korea has no nerves to speak of, but
any amount of abnormal appreciation of this
word "face".

Esson Third writes: "My neighbor across
the way has had about seventeen dogs snarling,
grinning, yelping, round his corn-stalk paling
for the last forty-eight hours. All the discordant sounds imaginable have been repeated a
million times. I inquired this morning as to
the neighbor and the neighbor's wife, of what
they were made—of wood, or mud, or dry
bones—that they could tolerate forty-eight
hours of such a pandemonium. My Korean
friends could not understand what I meant.
They understood the words but not the
thought. What had these dog noises to do
with the make-up of Mr. and Mrs. Chew.
Chew is at peace, Mrs. Chew is at peace as

Nerves
Unaffected by
Noise

well, both are in possession of unbroken face.
She has no diseased harp-strings in her soul,
that get all on edge with every noise that the
Orient gives off. I am struck with the difference between Mrs. Chew, for example, and
Thomas Carlyle. After forty-eight hours of
yelpings, snarlings, screamings, she is in perfect peace, and her soul reposes blissfully.
Carlyle had had one night of it at the hands
of a small dog over the way. He says, "By
five o'clock in the morning, I would have given
a guinea of gold for its hind legs firm in my
right hand by the side of a good stone wall."

**But Unable to
Bear Criticism**

Mrs. Chew, unmoved after forty-eight hours
of seventeen dogs, thinks what a diabolical
frame of mind for any man to be in. Carlyle
would die under this grinding of the nerves,
but to die because of what others thought failure he knew not. Nothing served better to
rouse the war-horse within him and his bris-
tling mane than to feel that he was the one man
against forty million other Britishers, "mostly
fools." Not so Korea.

**Loss of
"Face"**

In the recent political shipwreck the worst
is that Korea has gone down with loss of
"face". This is why Min suicided. This is
why the present brings a lonely shameful sense

of death to the people. Not the loss of tangible property so much as this ruin of the proper form, is what the Korean dies under. Humiliation unspeakable has gripped his soul, and he says: "With what face can I look upon the whole world, with what face will I meet the spirits of my forefathers in the Yellow Shades?"

However unreasonable this position may seem to be; how much better soever the present may seem as compared with the hopeless past, he views it not so. Friend Kim says, "Face is lost and eternal shame is my portion forever." At such a time as this, when he has written large over the portals of the future, *Chul-mang-mun* (the gateway of despair), "Abandon hope all ye who enter here," what a joy to be a missionary, called to such a time as this and to so needy a people to say to them: "Listen, while I read to you, 'Why art thou cast down, O my soul? And why are thou disquieted within me? Hope thou in God; for I shall yet praise him, who is the help of my countenance, and my God.'"

An Evangel of Hope

"Can he truly heal loss of face?" This is the question. Some think he can,—those who have tested him; some think he cannot,—

Reality of Divine Help

those who have not. One young man by the name of Wonderful, T. J. Wonderful, spoke in last Wednesday's meeting. He is a student twenty-two years old. He said: "I once looked with admiration upon a minister of state, I thought him the acme of all in all, till I learned God's message to my soul. When that came, the whole world changed; in place of admiration, there was nothing but a pitiful longing left, and a prayer that he too might believe. For a world of fallen countenances there is no help like God."

Power in
Alien Hands

Korea like all other nations loves power, power over the lives, destinies, and liberties of men. Millionaire kings are not seen here as at home, but official kings have always existed. Then too there are kings of literature and kings of ancient aristocracy. Power is sweet, but when one cannot have it, the next best thing is to look up and admire the man who has, if you consistently can. To-day power has passed out of the Korean's hand and into the hand of a man whom he cannot admire; hence there comes this feeling of desolation. Nominally power remains his still, but it is only the ghost and thin shades that we see.

A Contrast

In olden days tax-levying, collecting, disbursing, transmitting, and other details of administration, provided an unlimited field for the science of 'squeeze', and out of this grew one of Korea's most deadly national sins. To-day no taxes pass through the Korean's hand, except what he pays, or what he receives after permission of a Japanese official. This is the logical result of a long list of national wrong-doings, but it is bitter none the less. The yellow harvests of rice and the long stretches of beans and millet have lost their poetry, and are flat and colorless.

Then there was the field of office-seeking and appointing. Fierce were the tugs of war and glorious was the end to the victor with the spoils thereof. Happy the man who could ride down all opponents and get himself possessed of the two-handed paddle. To-day all this high privilege is in the hands of the Resident-General. To think of such a thing is like a nightmare from which he tries to shake himself into substantial awakening. He finds however that the dream is real, and that the desired reality is only a dream. _Office_

All educational matters, too, are in the hands of those who were once supposed to be illiterate island savages. They decide as to the course _Education_ of study, as to grants, as to grades of schools, as to teachers, as to everything that pertains to the world of letters.

Mining Privileges

The hills that were given Korea by God four thousand years ago, sown rich with gold and silver, have waited in vain for the miner's hand to dig them. Instead the Korean has peopled them with white and blue devils,[1] who threaten him with dire destruction if he dare cut into their backs or tails.[2] The result is, God has taken the hills away from him, and passed them on to others, and the Korean has no power to-day even to hold a mine, much less to grant concessions.

The Customs

The Customs, organized by Sir Robert Hart and developed by Sir John McL. Brown, are in the hands of the alien, too, and all the dollars that accrue therefrom.

The Military

The Korean soldier who used to stand guard by the Palace gates or drill out in the open square has been spirited away. He has gone, and not even the echo of his bugle-call remains to us. He was the nation's representative of power and glory, standing at present arms

---

[1] The "White Tiger" and "Blue Dragon" as named in geomancy.

[2] A street in Seoul still shows the Dragon's back protected by stones.

beautifully, or giving the general salute when the king went by. He is gone. The cicada-fly still sings, the tree-toad pipes, and the peasant quavers his old-fashioned throat notes of an evening, but "lights out" no longer greets the ear of the Korean soldier, and the reveille is silent. Only celestial armies, such as Elisha saw, fill the distant hills. Like a far-off whisper comes the word: "All power is given unto me in heaven and on earth. Accept my life. Swing into line with me, and all your doings will be victorious."

These have been bitter years. Hatred, suspicion, strife, with their accompaniments of bloodshed, burned villages, poverty, tears, and suicide, have cut deep into the souls of the people. Those whose hands were accustomed to the gentle methods of pipe and pen are to-day cold-blooded in the use of rifle, bayonet, and revolver. Every day the government papers report so many insurgents captured, so many wounded, so many shot. How men can hate, how they can lie and steal and murder, are old stories not to be learned in the East only. Who can pour oil on the troubled waters? Who can say to Galilee, when the typhoon bears across it, and blind with fury, drives Peter, John, and

Who is Sufficient?

their associates toward the grinding rocks, who can lift his hand at such a time and say, "Steady, cease!" Who can look on the man of failure, the man who has tried the sword and missed the mark, who has lied and sworn, and filled his heart with hatred and fear, a good-for-nothing, lost man, who by a look can melt such a one and bring him to his knees in tears of repentance? Who can say to prison doors, "Swing back", and to all of Caesar's guards, "Out of my way"? Who can speak and be heard by ears long dead? Who can turn a land of sorrow into glad rejoicing? Who can make me forget my wrongs, and love the man I hated, and make him whom I have wronged love me? Who can take zero and by multiplying it all down the ages make it spell infinity? Who can make out of poor Galilee drift-wood a being like Peter, almost divine? Who can bind together in one unbreakable bond of love Korea and Japan, and making them forget their mutual grievances, form of them a mighty people for the glory of his Father's name?

SUGGESTIVE QUESTIONS ON CHAPTER II

AIM: TO UNDERSTAND KOREA'S NEED IN HER NATIONAL HUMILIATION

I. *The National Humiliation.*

1. Why would the United States resent the proposal to choose a king as head of the nation?
2. Why would Canada resent the proposal to elect a President?
3. To what extent would this feeling on the part of the two nations be justifiable?
4. Why did the Koreans tolerate their corrupt and inefficient government?
5.* How near do you think their patriotism approaches that of Anglo-Saxon North America?
6. In what ways does it most markedly differ?
7. Why do the Koreans grieve so greatly over the loss of their reactionary king?
8. Why do they regret the passing of corrupt officials?
9. How would you feel if your country were garrisoned with foreign troops?
10. What is the difference between initiating reforms for yourself and having them dictated from without?
11.* Sum up as vividly as possible the Korean sense of national humiliation.

II. *The Needs of the New Order.*

12.* What are some of the differences in detail between a society founded on custom and one founded on the ideal of progress?
13.* What qualities are demanded for the second that are not necessary for the first?

14. What are the special dangers in the transition from the first to the second of these standpoints?

15. What are the disadvantages of a progressive society for a man who is not trained for it?

16.* What sort of training do you think Korean boys should have to fit them for the changing conditions?

17.* What sort of training should girls have?

18. What ideals of personal character does Korea need most just now?

III. *The Comfort of Christianity.*

19. Work out the points of resemblance between the present Korean political situation and that of the Jews in exile.

20. Select several passages from the Old Testament which you think would be of especial comfort to Koreans to-day.

21. In what respect was the political position of the early Christian Church like that of Korea at present?

22.* What things has the Christian Church to offer that help to supply the loss of nationality?

23. Collect the New Testament passages that you think would be most helpful in the present situation.

24. What is the message of the Bible on the subject of race hatred?

25.* What would be your counsel to a Korean patriot in the present distress?

REFERENCES FOR FURTHER STUDY,
CHAPTER II

I. *Recent History.*

Hulbert: The Passing of Korea, chs. VIII-XIV.
Bishop: Korea and Her Neighbors, chs. XXI-
XXIII, XXXI, XXXVI-XXXVII.
Gale: Korean Sketches, ch. XI.

II. *Korean Misrule.*

Hulbert: The Passing of Korea, ch. III.
Bishop: Korea and Her Neighbors, pp. 101, 102,
329, 446-448.
Gifford: Every-day Life in Korea, p. 57.

III. *Character of the King.*

Hulbert: The Passing of Korea, ch. XXVII.
Bishop: Korea and Her Neighbors, pp. 257, 258,
433.

THE BELIEFS OF THE PEOPLE

In no department of Korean life is the antiquity of their civilization so clearly demonstrated as in the mosaic of religious beliefs that are held, not only by different individuals, but by any single individual. We have no choice but to deal with these separately, but the reader must ever bear in mind that in every Korean mind there is a jumble of the whole; that there is no antagonism between the different cults, however they may logically refute each other, but that they have all been shaken down together through the centuries until they form a sort of religious composite, from which each man selects his favorite ingredients without ever ignoring the rest. Nor need any man hold exclusively to any one phase of this composite religion. In one frame of mind he may lean toward the Buddhistic element and at another time he may revert to his ancestral fetishism. As a general thing, we may say that the all-round Korean will be a Confucianist when in society, a Buddhist when he philosophizes, and a spirit-worshiper when he is in trouble. Now, if you can know what a man's religion is, you must watch him when he is in trouble. Then his genuine religion will come out, if he has any. It is for this reason that I conclude that the underlying religion of the Korean, the foundation upon which all else is mere superstructure, is his original spirit-worship. In this term are included animism, shamanism, fetishism, and nature-worship generally.

—*Homer B. Hulbert*

III

THE BELIEFS OF THE PEOPLE

Korea seems peculiarly devoid of religion. There are no great temples in the capital that tower above the common dwellings of men. There are no priests evident, no public prayings, no devotees, no religious fakirs, no sacred animals walking about, no bell-books or candles sold, no pictures with incense sticks before them, no prostrations, in fact no ordinary signs of religion, and yet if religion be the reaching out of the spiritual in man to other spirits over and above him, the Korean too is religious. He has his sacred books, he kneels in prayer, he talks of God, of the soul, of the heavenly country.

Outward Signs of Religion Lacking

We hear him repeat: "The man who does right God rewards with blessing; the man who does wrong God punishes with misery." "If we obey God we live; if we disobey him we die." "Secret whispers among men God hears as a clap of thunder; hidden schemes in the darkened chamber he sees as a flash of light-

Religious Sayings

ning." "Let the body die and die and die a
hundred times, and let all my bones return to
dust, and let my soul dissipate into nothingness,
yet not one iota of loyalty shall I change toward my sovereign lord [the king]."

**Superstition
Prevalent**

Korea's is a strange religion, a mixing of
ancestor worship with Buddhism, Taoism,
spirit cults, divination, magic, geomancy, as-
trology, and fetishism. Dragons play a part;
devils (*kwi-shin*) or nature gods are abundant;
tokgabi (elfs, imps, goblins) are legion and
are up to all sorts of pranks and capers; spirits
of dead humanity are here and there present;
eternal shades walk about; there are personali-
ties in hills, trees, and rivers, in diseases, under
the ground and in the upper air, some few
ministering to mortal needs, but most of them
malignant in their disposition, bearing wo and
terror to the sons of men. So easily are they
offended and so whimsical in their make-up
and difficult to please, that the spirit world is
little better than Hades let out of school, with
all mortals at their mercy. Hornets are hard
to fight against, as the kings of the Amorites
found in the days of Joshua; still a sure hand
may hit a hornet; but who among mortals can
overcome sprites, wraiths, and banshees, where

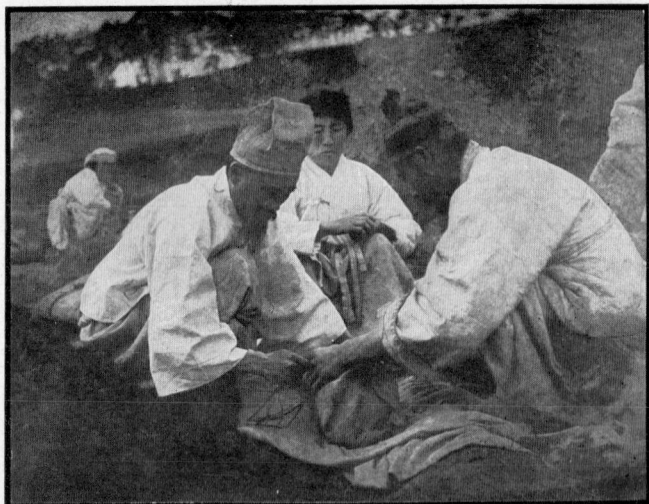

MOVING DEAD BODY THREE YEARS AFTER BURIAL BY ORDER OF GEOMANCERS

ANCESTOR WORSHIP

no head ever pops up or other visible appendage
accompanies?

But is there any religion that possesses the Ancestor Worship Holds Chief Place
heart of the nation as a whole, or are the people,
as Mrs. Bishop and Percival Lowell lead
one to infer, without anything of the sort?
The longer I am in touch with Korean environment the more emphatically would I say that
they have a religion, and that they do much
more for it, and because of it, than the average
Christians do at home for their faith.   High
above all other cults and customs stands Ancestor Worship.   It is the key-stone of Korea's
gateway to the happy lands of prosperity and
success.   To neglect it blocks the whole highway toward life and hope.   A good ancestor
worshiper may consult the Buddha, may inquire
of *Ok-wang Sang-je* (the Jade God of the Taoists), may bow or expectorate before the ordinary hill-gods, may set up posts to the Five
Point Generals, and consult luck and divination; but to forget the ancestors and to resort
to these only, would be to pray to the shadow
without the essence.   Ancestor worship possesses completely the heart and soul of Korea.

How does ancestor worship manifest itself, Its Outward Marks
seeing that there are no temples to remind one,

no altars, no shrines, no priests, no litany said
or sung? What are its marks or features? We
answer, the mourner's dress, the tablet, the
tablet-house, the grave. As these, and the
thoughts that accompany them, have occupied
a very much greater place in the life of Korea
than the tenets of the Christian faith have ever
done in any of the Western nations of the
world, I shall enter somewhat carefully into
their detail.

The Grave Site

A professional "earth-master" (*Chi-sa*),
ground doctor, tomb inspector, or whatever
you may call him, is summoned by the chief
of a house and asked to find a grave site for
the family. He is a father-confessor, but instead of pointing upward he points down. He
requires money too, the more the better, if the
family would be redeemed by his lucky find-
ings. He seeks out a quiet spur of a hill that
looks off toward enclosing peaks. There must
be no oozy waters, no noisy people, no nerve-
wearing winds, but the gentle breeze, the quiet
of the hills, and the full blessing of the sunshine. He sets his compass and then takes aim
from the different lines that radiate from the
center, to see what hill peaks show up, on the
right, or left, or in front. Lucky the site that

finds one along the compass line of posterity, for the family will then go on generation after generation; on the line of education, for then the house will be great as to scholars; along the line of rank, that many may be official kings; along the line of goods and chattels, so that every man may be wealthy. This is the heaven aimed at by the professor with his compass. When once found and proved satisfactory, he is paid off, and the grave is dug and plastered with lime, sand, and mud, and covered over ready for the departure of the father or mother or both.

When they die, wailing goes on for a time, **The Mourner** not gentle or smothered sobs, but open-mouthed howlings. In four days the members of the family are dressed in sackcloth, with ropes tied about the waist and head. All colors are set aside, as color denotes pleasure, joy, delight. The house is unswept and desolation reigns supreme, with wailings and self-denunciation. Envelope this in an atmosphere tainted by the presence of the dead, and you have a Korean demise and the accompaniments just as they ought to be. The mourner wears string shoes, never leather, for leather denotes ease and comfort; he eats no meat, holds no office, goes about with an umbrella hat on that hides the face of the sky from his guilty gaze. "Because of my transgressions my parents have died," says he, and when he writes a letter he signs it, "Yours truly, J. W. Kim, Sinner."

The Funeral

The corpse is dressed in finest silk, wrapped in hemp cloth, and then tied with three, sometimes four strips, the slit ends being fastened tightly round the body, which is then put into the coffin and covered. Books and articles specially prized by the deceased are often put in as well, and after a few days or months, as the case may be, the funeral goes out at night with lanterns burning and wailings of "*Aigo! aigo!*" Into such a discordant world as this come the words, "For if we believe that Jesus died and rose again, even so them also that are fallen asleep in Jesus will God bring with him."

The Soul

Each human being is supposed to possess two souls, one a male soul (*hon*), and one a female (*păk*). Naturally the male soul goes to heaven and the female to hell, while the body sleeps in the ancestral grave. There is no word of resurrection, for resurrection is over and above and outside of all the Confucian calculations.

Sacrifice

Sacrifice on the part of a Confucianist equals going to church, praying, entering the Sunday-

school class, joining in singing. To be the
head of a clan is more than to be a minister
or Sunday-school superintendent. For three
years, on the first and fifteenth of each month,
the head of the home offers rice, bread, beef,
Irish stew, greens, dates, chestnuts, walnuts,
persimmons, honey cakes, oil candy, and other
articles of food before the tablet which remains
in the room. The male soul comes down from
heaven on these occasions and inhales the fra-
grance and then goes back. The poor female
soul has no part therein. Wailing continues
for three months, and then the silent sacrifice
takes its place. It is observed each time at
midnight, or just before cockcrow. When the
tablet has been worshiped for three years, it
is put into the tablet-house, and mourning is
finished. Only three generations occupy the
tablet-house at one and the same time. When
a new spirit comes in, the tablet belonging to
the great-grandfather is taken out and buried.

On four or five special days of the year, sacrifice is offered early in the morning at the
grave, which becomes far more important than
the home of the living. A neighbor may en-
croach on the precincts of the living, and nothing result but a very noisy seance; but to

Requirements
Respecting the
Grave

invade the enclosure of the dead calls for the strongest arm of the law, the long paddle, the knife, the deadly potion, the fierce feud that goes on forever. The grave is cared for, watched and tended, combed and brushed, for the repose of the dead is all-important. If they be misplaced, the opposites of health, wealth, and happiness come to pass. A poor thin-faced consumptive came to the writer to have him help him move his mother's grave. "Where she lay was oozy with water, and I caught consumption," said he. "If I could but move her I'd get well." Poor lad, his hopes of life were centered in the situation of his mother's remains!

The Most Desperate Trouble

Let a thief at home kidnap a child and write the distracted parents, saying, "I have Nelly in my keeping; when you bring $500 to Smith's Corners at 1.00 A.M. and hand it over, you may have her back," and it would set the whole village by the ears. But suppose Pak the outlaw write to Min the millionaire, saying, "I've dug up your father's bones, and have them with me. If you send $5,000 at midnight to Long Valley Stream you may have them. If not sent by next full moon, be warned, I'll grind your ancestors' bones to powder." In this case, the extreme limits of desperation would be reached.

If one were to sum up the good and evil of the system, we might say that it is good in that it teaches children to reverence parents. There are no restive feelings on the part of a Korean son against his father's authority, for such a thing would be equivalent to rebellion against God. There is something noble and exalted in the choice of one's parents as divinities in default of a revelation from God. Surely highest on earth come the father and mother, higher than the hero of the Shintoist, higher than any intermediate beings whatever.

The Good in the System

The destructive influence of ancestor worship, however, far outweighs its benefits. It is a ruthless and voracious land-grabber; the best of the hills are for the dead. The living may go to Jericho, or may huddle together down in the malarial flats, while the ancestral shade rests in the high places on the hill. The exhilarating surroundings of trees and green sod are for the dead, the living are left to the dust and heat and smells of the market-place.

Its Destructive Influence

Ancestral piety forbids the digging of the hills for gold or silver or any other treasure. What are the living and what is yellow gold

Prevents Mining

compared with the sweet repose of my father's ghost? Away with all sordid visions and leave the hills in peace!

Impels to Early Marriages

Ancestor worship impels toward early marriages in its hurriedly reaching out after a new generation that will offer sacrifice to one's departed shade. Children are married off at ten years and sometimes less. Love marriages? What has love to do with it? There result, therefore, unhappy homes, concubinage, irresponsible parents, a score of families all huddled together in two or three little rooms, stupidity and misery untold.

Forbids Travel

The system forbids travel in this widely journeying age. If you are a good child, home you must come for sacrifice; no world-enterprise can interfere, a certain room, a certain plot of ground, a certain day, holds you fast prisoner. Some filial sons build a little shed out by the grave, and unwashed and uncombed take up their abode and exist there.

Causes the Spread of Disease

The uncleanness that goes with ancestor worship, the lack of bathing, the keeping of the dead remains long in the home, all minister to the spread of disease and to the promotion of epidemics which have worn down Korea since time immemorial.

Its extinction of woman is one of its most pernicious influences. She cannot sacrifice, she cannot carry down the family line. When she enters the world, disappointment announces her arrival, unless sons galore have preceded her. Her life is a life of submission, imprisonment, and burden-bearing. Her final destination is *Chi-ha* or *Whang-chun*, the Yellow Hell.

Depresses Woman

The end of all sacrifice is a people bound hand and foot, interfered with in office, hindered in travel, debarred from the use of the land that God gave them, impoverished and made unhappy by early marriages, walking, with gaze backward, more and more hopelessly into inextricable confusion, all in conflict with the age we live in. The twentieth century has no regard for ancestor worship, or ancestral hills, through which it goes on the railway train, around them, in front of them, cutting off luck and prosperity, screaming its wild note in the most sacred valleys, roaring like wild wheel-devils let loose.

It Must Be Discarded

Even if there were no Christianity to take its place ancestor worship must go. Out of the backs of the "blue-dragon" and "white-tiger"[1] come long lines of cars loaded with ore

Cannot Stand against the Modern Spirit

[1] Spirits supposed to reside in the hills.

that is fed into the mining stamps to be bitten and chewed and pulverized, till all the metal is extracted. The age rolling forward, as it is inexorably, is smoothing out all old superstitions and with them ancestor worship.

Course of the Missionary in Meeting It

Confronting the young missionary, in his ignorance, is the stupendous question of the ancestor, rooted deep in the generations that lie buried, and with its tentacles all about the living, associated with the wisest of the Orient, and backed up by the master (Confucius) himself and the sages. What can the young and often callow missionary do to meet this? Can he argue the point? Never. Can he speak of it at all with any effect? No. What can he do? Do as the negro did when he saw the black dog waiting guard at the gate, his jaw "big" and his eye "mighty dangersome". What did he do? He let him alone. Let it alone. Know all about it, but don't touch it. There is no need. Ancestor worship is dropped off by the spiritually alive, as the beggar drops off his old garments to become a prince imperial.

God

As mentioned before, the Korean talks of God. He is *Hananim,* the one Great One. His name in Chinese and also in Korean is made up of terms meaning "one" and "great." So he is the Supreme Ruler for whom there is no image or likeness in heaven or earth or under the earth. Greatness is his. Love and light and life and joy are not associated with him. I said to the old woman (not a Christian) dusting off the door-steps, "It will rain to-day." Her reply was "Rain? Who knows?" "But the morning paper says so under weather probabilities." "Morning paper? Dear me! What does the morning paper know about what Hananim will do?"

Immediately when the Bible is read, "In the beginning some One created the heavens and the earth", they answer, "Hananim." "Who is angry with the wicked every day?" "God." "The heavens declare the glory of Hananim; and the firmament showeth his handiwork." But to tell of Hananim coming down to this poor earth's manger, and living, suffering, dying, with the outcast and the lost, is a story, for the East, unreasonable, impossible, and yet a story that grips the heart and compels belief and acceptance. *His Revelation*

Koreans consult the Buddha sometimes. Buddhism has been here since 372 A. D. and its long course of history has been marked by various degrees of corruption and by dark *Buddhism*

deeds. In delightfully secluded corners and in
the shade and quiet of the hills are its temples.
So separated are they from the wicked world
and so shut away into the silent lands of medi-
tation and repose, that you would think them
the habitation of the holy, but it proves not to
be so. The phrase *Na-mu A-mi-ta-bul* is the
chief article of their creed, and their chief
forms observed are celibacy, vegetarianism,
and the non-taking of life. The Buddhist has
always been careful to have a shaved head in
a land of topknots and his bowing and manner
of speech differ from the ordinary "worldling"
(*sok-in*) as he calls him.

**Varying
Recognition**

The fall of the Koryu dynasty in 1391 A. D.
was supposed to be due to the corrupt influence
of Buddhism, and since then the state has
looked down upon it as an outcast religion.
No Buddhist priest was admitted within the
walls of Seoul for 500 years, and even to-day
the Confucianist uses the lowest and most dis-
respectful forms of speech to the Buddhist
wherever he meets him. Yet in times of
trouble, as when no son is born heir of the
family, or when worries or anxieties beset the
Palace, there come calls on the Buddha, and re-
quests that his priests pray. Many a time have

these seasons of prayer kept the writer awake at night—"*Om cha-ri chu-ri chun-je sa-pa-ha. Om man-hi pad-mi hum, om man-hi pad-mi hum.*" The priest knows not the meaning of what he says. They are set sounds that have passed down to him as propitious and lucky, and like a pent-up and bottled cask, once start the flow and he goes on with the most astounding rapidity seemingly forever and forever.

What shall we say in commendation of Korea's form of Buddhism? Perhaps it is that Sakyamuni has taught a lesson in tenderness and compassion. There is a gentleness in some of the old priests and a dreamy mystic something that inspires one to go softly, and to put all iron and hardness out of the soul. But Buddhism, with its gilded idols and its awful representation of the Ten Hells that await mortals and its unintelligible litany and its immoral priesthood, constitutes but a poor portal for the soul of man.

Influence and Value

Of Taoism there is almost nothing. Some few followers read the Old Philosopher. "The way that can be walked on is not the eternal way, the name that can be named is not the eternal name." Some in the spirit of this sect pray the long night through to find God,

Taoism

to get into touch with divinity. Our dear
brother, S. J. Keel, was once a Taoist. Chang-ja
one of the sages of this religion says: "The
number one man is unconscious of his body,
the spiritual man knows nothing of merit, the
holy man thinks not of his name." Here is a
verse of his, the opening poem in his book of
writings. It pictures the greatness of the
great as compared with the mediocrity of the
mediocre who are looking on.

> "There is a fish in the Great North Sea
>   Whose name is *Kon;*
>   His size is a bit unknown to me,
> Though he measures a good ten thousand *li*
>   Till his wings are grown,
> And then he's a bird of encrmous sail,
> With an endless back and a ten-mile tail,
> And he covers the heavens with one great veil,
>   When he flies off home."

A strange, dreamy, elfish, Rip Van Winkle
kind of doctrine is Taoism. Some scholars in
China think they find in its teaching a relation
to the Hebrew Bible and intimation of the
Trinity, but Koreans see no such resemblance,
and it is a dead cult as far as the peninsula is
concerned.

Shamanism

It must not be supposed, however, that ancestor worship occupies the whole spiritual

realm of Korea. It is the great religion of the
people; it is the essential belief of the orthodox,
the all-necessary form to observe and follow,
if one would be admitted to the society of the
holy. You are required to be an ancestor worshiper, but you are not required to be a spiritual
medium, or an exorcist, or a believer in hill
gods, or dragons, or divination, or star influences. Nevertheless the whole land is shadowed by these as was Egypt by the swarms of
locusts which came up to strip her. Mrs. Bishop
says demon-worship costs Korea one million
two hundred and fifty thousand dollars gold
per annum.[1]

A graphic and correct picture of spirit exist-
ences in Korea is touched off by the pen of
Dr. George Heber Jones: "In Korean belief,
earth, air, and sea are peopled by demons.
They haunt every umbrageous tree, shady ra-
vine, crystal spring, and mountain crest. On
green hill-slopes, in peaceful agricultural valleys, in grassy dells, on wooded uplands, by
lake and stream, by road and river, in north,
south, east, and west, they abound, making
malignant sport out of human destinies. They
are on the roof, ceiling, fireplace, kang, and

*Belief in
Demons*

---

[1] *Korea and Her Neighbors,* 403.

beam. They fill the chimney, the shed, the living-room, the kitchen, they are on every shelf and jar. In thousands they waylay the traveler as he leaves home, beside him, behind him, dancing in front of him, whirring over his head, crying out upon him from earth and air and water. They are numbered by thousands of billions, and it has been well said that their ubiquity is an unholy travesty of the Divine omnipresence. This belief keeps the Korean in a perpetual state of nervous apprehension, it surrounds him with indefinite terrors, and it may truly be said of him that he passes the time of his sojourning here in fear. Every Korean home is subject to demons, here, there, and everywhere. They touch the Korean at every point in his life, making his well-being depend on a series of acts of propitiation, and they avenge every omission with merciless severity, keeping him under the yoke of bondage from birth to death."

Revengeful
Spirits

The spirits of the dead who have passed from earth under some wrong or other, keep after the living till their wrongs are avenged a thousandfold. Many of them have not found a resting-place, neither in beast nor man, and so remain at large, more dangerous by far to

meet than even a striped man-eater. Terrors
untold accompany these vindictive spirits, who
are loose and on the warpath. Sickness, mad-
ness, poverty, disgrace, death, mark their
course. In each county there is a sacrificial
place set apart called *yo-dan,* where all the dis-
contented, displeased, distracted spirits are
wont to congregate and be sacrificed to. It is
a dangerous business, for any slip in the ceremony brings down the pack on the head of the
director of ceremonies. Again they are heard
crying at night; sometimes they become visible,
but usually they are hid from mortal view.
Some are big and some are little. Some guard
a whole village and have to be propitiated or
else they smite it with typhus and the like.
Some possess the hills and keep bit and bridle
on the tiger. If these hill gods be neglected
or insulted, they let loose their woes on the
market-place and we hear of children being
carried off and eaten or bitten by snakes, or
other mischances befalling them. There are
hill "bosses" or village "bosses" who are in
touch with the pit itself, and can call forth
legions on their own behalf.

Pan-su, or blind exorcists, ply their trade of   Exorcists
casting out demons. They possess themselves

of some great name, like that of George Washington, for example, and by its repetition and
the telling over of his sayings, out go the
devils. Then there are women called *Mu-tang,*
mediums who yield themselves up to some
demon or other, and then utter prophetic
words, or words that reveal mysteries.

Tokgabi

The *tokgabi* is half-demon and half-elf, always on the go, and up to all sorts of capers.
He will frequently cut off a Korean's topknot
when he is not looking, or walking peacefully
all unawares. The man is unconscious of it
till he feels the top of his head and says, "Hello,
who is it? Is it I or a Buddhist? Not a Buddhist? No, then I. Alack, the tokgabi has been
here and my topknot is gone." They push
covers inside of dishes, they throw sand against
the window-paper, they play with fire at night
out on the mountainsides.

Demon Posts

Here, there, and everywhere in Korea are
posts seen by the wayside, cut roughly with
grinning teeth, horrible face, and most fero-
cious eyes and ears. They are placed there to
keep devils from passing. Usually they are
called by the name of General, General this,
and General that. Frequently they stand in
pairs, side by side, or facing each other, one

ROYAL TOMB AND GUARDIANS

SPIRIT POSTS

the General and the other the General's wife. Down his front runs the inscription, "The General of Heaven," while down the front of his wife it says, "Mrs. General of Hell." These were the strong defense of Korea's poor people through the generations gone by against the countless forces of the unseen world.

The dragon is king of all scaled and crawl- The Dragon
ing creatures. He mounts high up to heaven, as when we see a waterspout; he goes down to the unfathomed depths of the deepest pool. He is a monster divinity, is the dragon. He exists under the hills, where his back is often protected by a pavement of stone, where the road is likely to cut into the quick. St. George may have slain him in England, but he flourishes in the Orient still. On Japanese coins is seen his clawy form twisted and mixed with many coils. On the Chinese flag he still breasts the breezes. In the most honored of Korean sacred books, *The Canon of Changes,* I read such a sentence as this: "The sixth line shows dragons fighting in the wild, their blood is purple and yellow." *Yong,* the dragon name, is in all mouths, from the king on the throne to the maid servant that is behind the mill.

Enough has been told to give the reader an A World of Fear

idea of the terrible world in which the Korean
has lived and lives. Every moment of his pilgrimage has been under the dominion of fear.
As was said before, he becomes a fatalist naturally, what comes to pass must come. His
birth-year, birth-month, birthday, birth-hour,
are in possession of the spirits, and they hold
them at their mercy, to toss about or worry as
the tiger does the unfortunate village dog that
has been caught napping.

Collective Spirit Host

Gather this world together as it has passed
the reader in review, and there will be the
ancestral spirits, mean enough and whimsical
beyond all reason, sufficient to make life a pilgrimage of awful suspense; but add to them
demons, goblins, elfs, dragons, hill-gods, and
what not and you have old Korea.

Gospel Picture of Christ's Power

Into this world comes the missionary with
his Book and its stories about demons. The
Korean reads and at once is attracted. Plenty
of demons in the New Testament, thousands of
them, but they are all on the run; down the
slopes of Galilee they go[1]; away from Christ's
presence they fly, till the blind sees and the soul
is lighted up[2]; hosts of them, howling devils[3];
and devils that shriek and foam at the mouth.[4]

---

[1] Matt. viii. 32.   [2] Matt. xii. 22.   [3] Mark v. 15.   [4] Luke ix. 39.

Never before in the history of Korea was the world of demons seen smitten hip and thigh. This Wonder-worker is omnipotent, for verily he has issued a reprieve to all prisoners, all who will accept of him, and has let them out of hell. Throughout the land prayers go up for the demon-possessed in his name, and they are delivered; prayers for healing, and the sick are cured; prayers for the poor, and God sends means.

His Omnipotence in Korea

Was there ever a land more needy, and where was a message ever dreamed of so miraculously suited to the need? Some of us have come East to learn how wondrously Jesus can set free the most hopeless of lost humanity. We have come to realize that there are demons indeed in this world, and that Jesus can cast them out; to learn once more that the Bible is true, and that God is back of it; to know that his purpose is to save Asia, and to do an important part of the work through young Americans, Canadians, Britons, and others, who will humbly bow before him and say, "Lord, here am I; send me."

Message Suited to the Land

SUGGESTIVE QUESTIONS ON CHAPTER III

AIM: TO APPRECIATE THE INSUFFICIENCY OF KOREA'S
RELIGION TO MEET THE NEW NEEDS

I. *The Good and Evil of Ancestor Worship.*

1. Name all the good points that you can find
   in ancestor worship.
2.* Should an effort be made to incorporate any
   of these points in Korean Christianity? If
   so, how?
3. What effect would it have upon real reverence for the dead to imagine that the position
   of a grave might bring disease to the living?
4. To what extent should reverence for the dead
   be allowed to interfere with business and
   travel, and to what extent not?
5. What recommendation or criticism have you
   for the relations of parents to children in
   Korea?
6.* In what ways does ancestral worship affect
   the position of woman in society?
7.* Do you think that missionaries are justified
   in refraining from all attacks upon ancestor
   worship? Defend your views.

II. *The Mental and Moral Confusion of Superstition.*

8.* Try to think out in detail what practical difference it would make in your life if you
   really believed in the existence of imps and
   spirits.
9. What possible defense would you have if evil
   spirits attacked you?
10. What effect would a belief in spirits have

upon a man's resoluteness in confronting
difficulties?

11. What effect would it have upon plans for the
future?

12. In what way does this belief stand as an obstacle to science?

13. What evils arise from attributing every mis-
fortune to the arbitrary displeasure of some
spirit?

14. What do you think would be the relative value
of the scientific and religious method in com-
bating the belief in spirits?

15.* Sketch the line of argument that you would
employ in dealing with believers in evil
spirits.

III. *The Message of Christianity.*

16. How would you utilize the Korean idea of
Hananim in teaching Christianity?

17. Where would you expect to find your greatest
difficulty in using this idea?

18. Contrast the message of Buddhism and Christianity for a nation in political distress.

19. Contrast the external and public manifestations of Protestant Christianity with those of
religion in Korea. What elements are most
peculiar to each?

20.* What principal needs of Korea in the way of
institutional and social life will Christianity
supply?

21.* How will Christianity remove the evil and
supplement the good of Korean life?

REFERENCES FOR FURTHER STUDY
CHAPTER III

I. *Ancestor Worship.*

Gifford: Every-day Life in Korea, ch. VI.
Gale: Korean Sketches, pp. 215, 216.
Underwood: The Call of Korea, pp. 79-81.
Noble: Ewa: A Tale of Korea, pp. 57-60.

II. *Spirit Worship.*

Hulbert: The Passing of Korea, ch. XXX.
Bishop: Korea and Her Neighbors, pp. 290, 399-426, 443, 444.
Gifford: Every-day Life in Korea, ch. VIII.
Underwood: The Call of Korea, pp. 85-94.
Noble: Ewa: A Tale of Korea, pp. 49-53.

SOCIAL LIFE AND CUSTOMS

Woman's rights are few and depend on custom rather than law. She now possesses the right of remarriage, and that of remaining unmarried till she is sixteen, and she can refuse permission to her husband for his concubines to occupy the same house with herself. She is powerless to divorce her husband, conjugal fidelity, typified by the goose, the symbolic figure at a wedding, being a feminine virtue solely. Her husband may cast her off for seven reasons— incurable disease, theft, childlessness, infidelity, jealousy, incompatibility with her parents-in-law, and a quarrelsome disposition. She may be sent back to her father's house for any one of these causes. . . . Domestic happiness is a thing she does not look for. The Korean has a house, but no home. The husband has his life apart; common ties of friendship and external interest are not known. His pleasure is taken in company with male acquaintances and *gesang;* and the marriage relationship is briefly summarized in the remark of a Korean gentleman in conversation with me on the subject, "We marry our wives, but we love our concubines."

--Isabella Bird Bishop

"Before Christ came into our home," said one of our native Christian women, "I never knew what it was to eat a meal in the same room with my husband. His meals were served to him in the *sarang* (reception room), while I had mine on the earth floor of the kitchen. He always spoke to me in the lowest grade of servant talk and often called me by insulting names. Sometimes when he was angry or drunk, he used to beat me, and my life was as miserable as that of most all the heathen Korean women. But now that Christ has come into our hearts, everything is changed. My husband has not struck me once since he became a Christian. We have our meals and prayers together in the sarang, and now he always speaks kindly to me, addressing me as an equal. The past life was a bad dream; the present is a foretaste of heaven. We did not know what love was until Christ came into our home to teach us."

—George Heber Jones

IV

SOCIAL LIFE AND CUSTOMS

Society has rested on five strong pillars, The *Oh-ryun,* or Five Laws called *Oh-ryun.* They were chiseled out of ancient marble, by unknown hands, in prehistoric times, and have stood high through all the ages, holding the four corners of the Eastern world, and propping up the middle beams thereof. The Five Laws they are sometimes called, and on them rests the world of Confucius. Recently a Mr. Yi Wung-geung, a Christian, and one of Korea's most noted scholars, has written a reader for girls, and in the opening chapter he begins: "The doctrine of men rests on the Five Laws. Between father and son it requires *chin* (friendship) ; between king and courtier, *eui* (righteousness) ; between husband and wife, *pyul* (deference) ; between old and young, *saw* (degree) ; between friends, *shin* (faith)."

Allied to these are the Five Virtues, *in, eui,* The Five Virtues *ye, chi, shin,* or love, righteousness, ceremony, knowledge, faith. Herein the whole of superior teaching was summed up, and concerning these millions of pages have been written, and armies of Chinese characters have been called into requisition to tell all that was to be told. *In-eui-ye-chi-shin* is pronounced as one word, and all the people use it. The coolie as well as the statesman or gifted man of letters says, *"In-eui-ye-chi-shin"*. Any nation exemplifying it is civilized and any failing to observe it is barbarous.

The Five Elements

Another five must be called in, and then we shall have the fifteen that round out the circle. These are the Original Elements, metal, wood, water, fire, earth, *keum-mok-su-wha-do,* also a single word in its frequency of use and wideness of application. These are called the *Oh-hang,* and what is there that cannot be explained by them? The *Oh-ryun* (Five Laws), the *Oh-sang* (Five Virtues), and the *Oh-hang* (Five Elements) govern the Korean world of thought. The Five Elements serve as foundation, the Five Laws as the pillars, and the Five Virtues as the firmament above.

A Faithful Son

These might be designated the soul of Korean society. How many stories are told to illustrate the Five Laws! For example, such and such a lad was good to his feeble

mother, and faithful in bowing before his
father's grave. He was dogged by every circumstance of evil; poverty was after him with
hungry eyes; winter was upon him, biting cold;
sickness and ill luck tried him to the bitter
end; but through it all he cared for the needy
one, and walked daily through the snow to the
mound on the hillside. As a reward for such
virtue, an angel appeared to him, crowned him
with high honor, and pronounced wealth and
happiness his forever. He married a beautiful
princess, had untold riches and many sons, and
was happy ever afterward.

A set of five readers prepared some hundred
years ago, abound in such stories. Undoubtedly a strong steadying influence has been exer-
cised on the state and on society by the observ-
ance of the Oh-ryun, so that courtiers have
been loyal, children filial, wives faithful, age
honored, and friendship sacred.

Influence of the Five Laws

To illustrate the Five Virtues, love, righteousness, ceremony, knowledge, faith, let
one story suffice, written by a governor of
north Korea, one hundred and fifty years
ago. "In the late autumn a peasant caught
two wild geese, clipped their wings, and gave
them to me. I kept them in the court, where

Wild Geese Illustrating the Classic Virtues

the steward looked after them. One day he came to me and said, 'These birds are better-flavored than quail or pheasant; I advise your excellency to kill and eat.' 'Kill and eat? Out on you, man,' said I, 'Have you never noticed wild geese, how they fly, for example? They preserve the strictest *ye* (ceremony, order); when they mate there is no disorder or impropriety, they understand *eui* (what is right); in their migrations they follow the warmth of the sun, they have *chi* (wisdom); though they come and go you can always count on their passing at the right time, that is *shin* (keeping faith); they never make war on other creatures with bill or claw, that borders on *in* (love). It is a bird of the sacred classics, and would never do to make soup of like chicken or quail.' "

Relation of the Elements to Life

As to the Oh-hang—metal, wood, water, fire, earth—they play a most important part in all the affairs of life. They underlie everything, are the foundation in fact, not only of material things, but of domestic life and spiritual existence as well. In the case of a marriage they are anxiously called in, shuffled, and consulted. If a young man whose element is wood is mated to a metal girl, he will suffer as wood does from ax and saw and chisel. If he be married to a fire girl, nothing but total destruction awaits him. Earth and water are the only safe elements with which wood can mate. All the domestic unhappiness of olden time was explained on the principle of the Five Elements and bad mating. To say that the Oh-hang enters into every detail of life is scarcely putting it too strongly.

Society, based on, built up, and covered by these sets of laws, got itself into a fixed and immovable condition. The compass of the law governing was so small, and the conditions enclosed so multifarious, that no independent move could be taken by any one member of society without disturbing all of the others. "As it was, is now, and ever shall be," was written large over all things Korean; every wheel in the brain was stopped except those moved by Oh-hang, or Oh-ryun, or Oh-sang. Independent thought was not dreamed of. Korea has scored no invention, no discovery, no advance, in a thousand years. Backward, ever backward the nation has gone, little by little, in its unconscious existence, saying over and over to itself: "As it was, is now, and ever shall be; as it was, is now, and ever shall be."

A Fixed Social Condition

Whether in architecture, or in education, or in dress, or in other affairs of life, custom rules. Custom explains everything.

"What about this absurdity?"

"Oh, it's custom."

"Yes, but see here, why are the dead propped up on sticks and not buried?"

"Oh, it's custom."

"Do you sometimes marry off children as early as nine years of age?"

"Yes, that's custom."

The reader must learn this word if he would understand old Korea, and if he would read into much of the life of the East still. The forefather may have been an imbecile, or may have walked in his sleep, but what he did has come down, down to the present, and custom maintains that it is the sane and right thing to do.

"Why do you feed all these idle tramps, who come calling at your door, and you a poor man?" I once asked of my host.

He replied "It's custom, and for my life I can't get out of it."

"What about these dolmens set up all through these valleys here like tables of the gods, what do they mean?"

"They were set up by the Chinese invader, thousands of years ago, to crush out the ground influence that brought forth Korean warriors."

"You mean that they have stifled out the life of the nation for all these centuries?"

"Yes."

"Then why don't you roll them off and get back your lost vigor?"

"Oh, that's no use now, never do."

"As it was, is now, and ever shall be," is the only reply.

In Korea the most distressing condition of all was this strangling of independent thought. There was ceremony, gentleness, deference, kindness, appreciation of fun and humor, but for comparison and conclusion and action there was no room. One longed to drill a hole into the brain, pour in oil or anything that would lubricate, and set the wheels moving. They are moving now, however, and some of them with fine freedom. An Edison may little by little come forth from the shadows and be born, but for three thousand years it was as impossible to bring forth such as he as for a scrub pine to grow glorious persimmons.

A Stifled World

We shall look for a moment at the home life, ever remembering these bands of iron and

The Head of the Family

brass. The father is the lord high executioner. The Oh-ryun says that he shall be revered almost as a god by his posterity. He is greater even than the king. What he says is law, and what he does must be acknowledged respectfully and agreed to. While the majority of Korean fathers are kind to their children, custom paints him a Nebuchadnezzar with a fiery furnace prepared for other members of the household. He talks in terms of command to all others about him, as we might say in English, "Come here. Go there. Sit down. Stand up. Bring my pipe." The Korean language is rich in tones and expressions of high command, and the father is a past master of the whole subject. When you live near him, watch his daily life, and catch the accents of his voice, you think of Sitting Bull, the Turkish Sultan, the Grand Vizier, the Czar, and yet none of these seem quite to describe him.

He says, "There's John now, he's three months old; I must look sharp and get him betrothed." He calls in a go-between and after various seesawings, consulting of Oh-hang, and casting of lots, John is betrothed, sometimes to a girl baby, sometimes to one already six or seven years old. John is not interested. He

sleeps hard on the matting and awaits his fate.
Mary is married off likewise. Years later,
when the wedding-day comes, neither one nor
other thinks of entering a protest or of saying,
"Why was I not consulted?" John grows up
to be just the same as his father, gives his
commands like a sea-captain from the bridge,
and settles his son before his mother knows
what he looks like. Thus are the children
dealt with.

As for the wife, when time wears on her and
her cheek grows wan and faded, her lord high
executioner calls in another woman to share
the fortunes of the home. The wife bows in
humble submission, and uses high and respectful language in acknowledging this new order
of affairs. No wonder girls in Korea are sorry
to be born a member of their sex, and every
boy walks in high hopes of his innings coming
later.

The Wife

The woman's place is, first as daughter, one
of contempt. A missionary's little six-year-old
once came to him with tears in her eyes and
said:

How Daughters Are Viewed

"Papa, I have a question."

"Yes, what is it?"

"Are you sorry that I wasn't a boy?"

"Well I should say not, I wouldn't trade you for a dozen boys. But why do you ask?"

She said, "The Koreans were talking just now, and they pointed at me and said, 'What a pity that she wasn't a boy!'"

At the Period of Marriage

The Korean woman is married at last, but not with any high hilarity such as attends wedding-days at home. She goes with blood-red marks painted on her face, and her eyes sealed, like a wooden doll, turned this way and that, stood up, set down, moved here and there, pulled and pushed through all the wooden ceremony of marriage, till at last she emerges daughter-in-law, with three powers set over her head, husband, mother-in-law, and father-in-law. Young wives are not always unhappy, but it is no thanks to custom or circumstance that they are not.

The Mother

The mother is an important member of the family in her relation to children only. If she has no son, alas for her! better had she never been born. Not only is she condemned by her husband and every member of the clan, but she condemns herself, and no ray of sunshine ever gladdens her broken soul. She is Rachel, and Hannah, and Elizabeth, as they were before joy visited them. In this matter

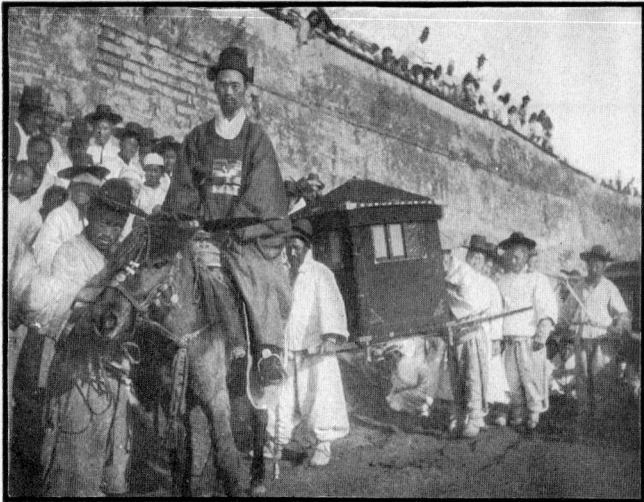

GROOM RETURNING WITH HIS BRIDE

BRIDAL FEAST AFTER THE CEREMONY

the spirit of the opposite seems to rule from
that of the West.   Happy the woman who has
a great circle of posterity to look down upon.
"Who is the most noted woman in Europe?"
asked the childless Madame de Stael of Na-
poleon.   "She who has reared the largest
family," was the sharp reply, and Korea would
say, "Amen."

Woman is a useful member of society, for
material interests hang on her hand.   Once,
on a walk by the city wall, we saw a man sitting on a stone weeping.   His was a full-
mouthed, heart-broken cry, as though the
world had given way under him.   "Why,"
we asked.   "Why all this fuss?"   He looked
vacantly at us for a moment, and then resumed
where he had left off.   We found that the
trouble was about a woman, his wife, she had
left him.   "How he must have loved her to cry
like that," remarked a lady in the party.   It
was translated, but he resented it, "Loved her?
I never loved her, but she made my clothes and
cooked my food; what shall I do? boo-hoo-oo,"
louder and more impressively than ever.

Thus was, yes, and still is, the world of
woman, but mighty changes are taking place,
and underneath the framework of her prison-

*Woman's
Service in
Material Things*

*Changes and
Her
Emancipation*

house earthquakes are shaking. She is to be free, but what will her freedom mean? Confucius never guessed the place of woman in society, he missed the mark as widely as the Russians did in the battle of Tsushima. Jesus, in the face of all the ages that spoke opposition, placed her where God would have her and there by his grace she stands. She has been the slave, the dog, the toy, the chattel, the convenience of men, for all past ages. Now new voices are heard proclaiming that she shall be free.

The Family Circle

The family exists but not the circle. There is no table around which they gather for meals, no reading nor music, no evening parties which draw them together, no "At Homes", no family pew in which to sit on Sunday, no picnic excursions in which all members join. The master eats by himself, the wife by herself, the sons and daughters each separately and alone. Because of this, our custom of conversing at table, and allowing the talk and attention to wander all over the universe, while semiconsciously engaged in the serious act of "eating rice," seems very absurd. "When you eat, eat, and when you talk, talk, but why try both at one and the same time?"

Korean homes are in a sense open to all the **No Privacy**
world. Any one who pleases may try the door,
push it open, and come in. He needs no first
acquaintance, and no introduction. An ordinary Korean guest-room is free to all the world.
On the other hand the inner quarters are sep-
arate, and for a male traveler to venture there
would be a breach of the most sacred law of
society. Into this outer room, come gentlemen of leisure, tramps, fortune-tellers, Buddhist priests, all mankind, in fact. Here is
located the high seat of the master. As you
live in this guest-room, you feel the fearful
lack of privacy. You are as though encamped
on the open highway, under the gaze of all
men. If you write a letter, the question is,
to whom are you writing it. "Why do you
write thus and thus? What reference is here?
Who? When?" These are the questions that
are asked by those who look over your
shoulder, without any breach of proper form
or infraction of the eternal law that governs
things.

It becomes a question sometimes with the **An Ordeal to the**
young missionary as to how much he can stand **Missionary**
of the search-rays of the human eye, and if
he does break down what form the break-

down will take. In the early days especially, from chinks and corners came these never-ceasing search-lights. This is the East; it was born so, raised so, and lives so, unconscious of the burden of it.

Unreasonable-ness

The regular laws of cause and effect seem to be out of gear on this side of the 180th meridian. Medical practise is unreasonable. If you have a pain, a long darning-needle is stuck into you to relieve it. If you have an inner sickness, the doctor will ask you a question or two, then he will multiply earth by fire and divide by wood, and the result will be a mixture fit for the witch's caldron, and this you are expected to steep and drink from. To us it seems very unreasonable. Still, we, on our side, to them are as much out of touch with their fitness of things as they to us.

An Illuminating Conversation

Recently a conversation between two Koreans, Yi and Kim, ran thus:

"I'll tell you the reason, Kim, that we Koreans do not make as good soldiers as the Japanese, it's because we are no hands at shutting one eye and keeping the other open. You must shut one eye, you know, to aim," and Yi screwed up his face into a twisted knot to get his one eye to close, but it was in vain.

"Nothing of the kind," replied Kim, "I can shut one eye and leave the other open as much as I please."

"Then let me see you do it," said Yi, all the time trying frantically to get his one eye to close properly.

"No trouble about it," said Kim, rubbing the ink on the inkstone and then dipping his brush and tasting it.

"Then I ask you to do it, let me see you shut one eye now and leave the other open."

"I could do it if I had a gun," said Kim.

"Oh, yes," said Yi, "You could do it if you had a gun, but you can't do it if you haven't, and the Japanese can."

One of the curses of Korean society is debt, **Debt** and the persistency with which all people run therein. Every man would seem to owe the other. A clear statement, with all paid off and none due, seems never to have been heard of. Borrowing and paying huge interest has been the custom. Twenty years ago it was 12 per cent. a month. Little by little it has fallen till to-day it is 4 or 3 or 2 per cent. monthly, the lowest on record.

Here is a note from the *Seoul Press*, written **Unduly Generous** in 1906: "Koreans are not misers; they are spendthrifts. Money glides by them and goes easily the way of all the earth. Every man aims to be rich, in order that he may have cash to spare; and nothing pleases him better than to part with it for a friend, in hospitality and good fellowship. Are they poor people or are they rich? No man knows. They have little money for necessities, but any amount for luxuries. Americans would quarrel over a mite that Koreans would scorn to speak of. His relative over the way, the Chinaman, is a loathsome miser in comparison. The Korean will be hard up always and yet never break his pace as a gentleman of leisure. If I were poor, and had no means, and was obliged to throw my remaining days on the generosity of the public for food and clothes and comfort, I should appeal to the Korean, knowing that he would never see me want, would be respectful while generous, and would never be so mean as to cast up my good-for-nothingness to me."

Habitual Kindness and Official Cruelty

The Koreans are a kind-hearted people. Those of us who have gone in and out among them for nearly a quarter of a century can vouch for it. No more gentle or hospitable race exists, and yet there have been through its history fearful outbreaks of cruelty, and traces of these remain till to-day. If a man sinned against the state, the innocent women of his household suffered and the little children as well.

In the troubles of 1885 an old conservative gentleman lived near the East Gate. When the names of the movers of the riot were published, his son's name stood high up on the list. Seeing this, he went into the inner room, called his little grandchild and said, "Alas! we have lived to be disgraced, you by your father and I by my son. We shall die together." So he and the little laddie drank the hemlock, and made atonement for the son.

Making Atonement

There is no individual in society, it is one body corporate. If one member sin all suffer with him. The fearful forms of torture loom up yet out of the shadows, the paddle, the rack, the chair, the cangue collar, the strangle-ring, the shin-rod, and various forms of mutilation remind one of what we see in the Tower of London. Truly we are brethren in cruelty if we go far enough into the dark past. But God who is rich in mercy, when he transforms an Oriental, seems first of all to take out of his heart the poison of cruelty, and to leave the spirit of self-sacrifice and tenderness instead.

Mutual Suffering

Lack of Hygiene

"For the public weal" has never until recently cut any figure in Korean society. All common interests were left to the other person. Roads, as we have said, go where they like and as they please. Garbage-carts and wagons and a garbage-heap miles away from the city do not exist. The refuse heap is just outside the front gate, and the kite birds and the summer rains are the scavengers. The streets become the backyards heaped high, and travelers through Ping yang and Seoul get a fearful view of Korean life, seeing the very worst possible from the very first. Odors abound and epidemics are rife, but long usage has hardened those passing by, and the olfactory nerves no longer respond to this high vibration.

Mr. Yi and the Mummy

It recalls to the writer Mr. Yi, consul-general and minister, who was once walking through Central Park Museum, New York. We reached the mummy chamber, and Mr. Yi gave one look at them and took firm hold of his nose. "Why do you hold your nose?" was the question asked. Without letting go his hold he pointed with the other hand at a mummy. "But he has been dead for five thousand years." "Has he?" said he, taking a firmer grip. He would not have noticed one of these fearfully unkempt streets, but the supposed scent of the mummy he could not tolerate.

Korea is clean in dress, however, and this makes the land a paradise when compared with Chefoo, China, for example. The frequent bathing that one sees in Japan does not exist, but the immaculate suits that are donned at every short interval, even by the poor, go far to make amends.

Immaculate Dress

Society as a body has been blind and deaf and dumb. There have been no public gatherings, no public opinion audible, and no eye that could see for the many. Christianity comes gently but persistently, step by step, in at all gateways. One of its marks is that it can speak, it is peculiarly a voice; it can see, and can control the eye. Through its good news society is awaking to see and to hear and to speak.

Society Becoming Conscious

Society is so interlocked and bound together by the patriarchal system that, not only is independent thought out of the question, but there is no room for patriotism, no room for sincerity, no place for accuracy. Chief among the many fathers, is the father of the family. Then there is the father of the state, the king, and as the father of the family has power ab-

System of Patriarchal Authority

solute within the limits of his own home, so
in state affairs the king is absolute. Human
life and honor hang on his hand. "Exalt him,"
reads the command, and behold the man is
exalted. "Take him out and behead him," and
lo, the man, without trial or chance for his life,
dies.

**Several Present
and Past
Embodiments**

Then there is the provincial father or magis-
trate. He too within a narrower circle is absolute, and can reprimand and order and be-
rate as he pleases. Then there is the literary
father, the schoolmaster, once greatly held in
esteem, now fallen amid the debris of ancient
systems and ideals. There are many other
fathers, all of whom hold sway within their
own sphere.

**No
Independence
of Thought**

Such being the case, independence of thought
or action is out of the question. Do, I must,
as all others have done, safe-guarding the Oh-
ryun, exalting the Oh-sang, and using the Oh-
hang to help keep my bearings. When a new
set of conditions arise that are not already
provided for, the Korean is at sea. He is con-
fronted by the dress problem these days, for
example, and scoop hats and pole-stick skirts
are coming on. He has never had any freedom
in action heretofore, and suddenly he has fallen

heir to it without preparation. Knowledge under any condition is the result of experience, so that even a sage in the classics may be but a child when it comes to baking bread or gardening.

For generations the Korean has walked by instinct and not by reason. Every possible circumstance was provided for, and all he had to do was to shut his eyes and let himself go. But new conditions and a new world have come crashing into his ancient domain, and where is he? Esson Third says: "The other day an unsophisticated Korean was riding on a through train from Fusan, the fast express going at thirty miles an hour. For a time it amused and interested him to look about the painted wagon beneath which the landscape seemed to be racing in all directions. He looked at this and examined that, and finally grew tired of the inside of the car and poked his head out of the window to see how the world wagged. A gust of wind carried off his hat and hat-string, and away it went sailing down the valley. He shouted, 'My hat,' but the wagon made no response. In an instant he was at the door, out onto the platform, and before you could think, head first he went down

Facing New
Conditions

over the embankment after that hat. We saw no more of him, but I imagined a pitiful bundle low in the valley, a mixture of white clothes, black topknot, and brown honest face, fearfully crumpled over his plunge after a five cent hat." Here were a new set of conditions, and he acted in his old way, by instinct instead of reason.

An Impulsive Interrogatory

Another Korean sat on the open platform of a construction train. The day was warm and he nodded in deep sleep. He was a man of the world, had seen much, and knew how to ride on railway trains. Deep was the nod and comfortable the sleep, but a curve met them around which the train whip-lashed violently, and away went this son of the Orient over the edge, down the green bank over and over till he reached the bottom. In an instant he was on his feet, wide awake, with a flash in his eye and a look at the train that said, "What in creation do you mean?" This circumstance also was new, and the thought called forth was an impulse rather than a conclusion.

Patriotism

With these laws governing, and customs binding round and round, and fierce ancestors standing as if on guard with shotgun, there has been no room for patriotism. "Keep your hands off Cæsar and all that pertaineth to him," has been a rule of life for old Korea. The principal association that went with government was the long knife, the cangue collar, the paddle, the shin-rod, and other instruments of punishment.   Patriotism therefore is a new product, and as yet somewhat abnormal in its character and growth.

Korea has lived in an atmosphere of fear. **Fear** When you could be arrested and beaten at the will of state father or provincial father, just when the whim might take him, what room was there for a long easy breath? The same writer quoted above says: "Koreans are all more or less cowards.   Why should they not be so, living as they do without any confidence in anybody, ignorant of everything, and threatened all the time by ten thousand evil influences? They have no idea of standing together or of organizing, and are just beginning to hear the mysterious words, 'liberty, equality, fraternity'."

In olden days the standard of education was **Lack of** that derived from China, to-day it is mathe- **Accuracy** matics. The Korean has come suddenly on a new vein, and is digging like a "forty-niner" to possess all of its treasure.   Until the present time a lack of accuracy has been one of Korea's characteristics. A writer in the *Seoul Press* says: "Time was nothing, day after to-morrow was just the same as the day before yesterday. A promise fails, not because men are dishonest, but because no one ever dreams of being exact in anything. In Korea a definite description is impossible, and exact information is out of the question. Hard and fast accuracy of statement does not get within signaling distance of the Korean's soul. He cannot understand what you mean by it. The newly arrived missionary physician says to the interpreter: 'Tell the patient to shake the bottle and take one half teaspoonful half an hour after meals, in a wine-glass of water'. The interpreter says: 'Shake the jug, and take a good lot of the mixture five or six times a day till you feel better'."

A Fatalist   The Korean, shorn of independent action and riveted to this machine called society, is an out-and-out fatalist. His Eight Characters settle his destiny. God the distant, all-powerful, unapproachable One has his life in his keeping. His Oh-hang are always after him. What happens must happen, when he falls he must fall, if he's poor he must be poor, when

he dies he dies. His being has no play
inside of the tight clamps that grip him round
about. His belief in the fearful law of *Unsu*
possesses him. If he fails in business it is
Unsu; if he is dirty and miserable it is Unsu;
if the state falls, no one is to blame, for no one
can withstand Unsu. In a recent public lec-
ture the Hon. T. H. Yun, who is both a Westerner and a Korean, said to those before him:
"Until you give up the word Unsu, there is no
hope. It is nonsense, there is no such thing.
Every man is his own Unsu, and can make
of life what he will."

Underneath this social structure with its Oh- **Social Upheaval**
ryun and Oh-sang and Oh-hang great charges
of dynamite are exploding. They have come
about through the opening of the gates, the
incoming of the missionary, and the invasion
by Japan. This country's ideals, so different
from and so diametrically opposed to those of
old Korea, are upon us, and a great smashing
up of all the social system is taking place.

Has the gospel anything to offer at such a **Startling Gospel**
time as this? When the old paternal system **Truths**
has given way and domestic life and government are at sea, it comes in tones of matchless
simplicity and says: "Our Father, who art in

heaven, thy kingdom come. In the Father's house are many mansions, prepared for those that love him." How about *in-eui-ye-chi-shin?* The character *in,* is made up of men and two, two men, showing that love always keeps in mind the other one; but chief of all altruistic teachers is the Word of God, and it comes with its message to take the place of the lost virtue, *in.* *Eui,* righteousness, is made up of sacrificial lamb, and first personal pronoun, I. I, underneath the sacrificial lamb, means righteousness. My oneness with Jesus not only takes the place of the character, but fills out its thought, and makes the studies of the past a prophetic voice pointing to the great revelation.

Freedom

Where is freedom to be found, freedom from past bondage, from present bondage, from the bondage of self, from custom, from fear, from superstition? The heart of the nation these days goes out in longings for freedom. "Ye shall know the truth, and the truth shall make you free." Korea's ancient civilization appears to be a planned opening of the way for receiving the gospel at the present day; and the reader will doubtless be able to see through its bondage a groundwork for present hope.

SUGGESTIVE QUESTIONS ON CHAPTER IV

AIM: TO APPRECIATE THE NEW NEEDS OF KOREAN
SOCIETY

I. *The Ideals of Korean Society.*

1. Which of the five laws seem to you most, and
   which least ideal as to relationships?
2.* Name what you consider the five principal
   virtues for mankind, and compare them with
   the Korean list.
3. Compare the five Korean virtues with the
   fruits of the Spirit, mentioned in Galatians
   v. 22-23, and note the most striking differences.
4. Compare them with the two great command-
   ments given by Christ.
5. What do you consider the most notable omis-
   sions in the list of Korean laws and virtues?
6. What would you infer as to a system that
   made ceremony one of its five cardinal
   virtues?

II. *The Rule of Custom.*

7. What effect will the Korean power of custom
   have upon the character of the virtues developed?
8. What classes profit most from a social order
   based on custom, the superior or the inferior?
   Illustrate your answer from the position of
   the woman and child in Korean society.
9.* What are the advantages and what the disadvantages of a society in which custom is all-
   powerful?
10. What is its effect upon personal development?

11. What is its effect upon public progress?

12.* What have been the different ideals of Korean and American education?

13. What ideals of American education are most needed in Korea?

III. *Changes Needed in Family Life.*

14. What have been the advantages and disadvantages of giving the father of the family such absolute control?

15.* Name in the order of their importance the changes you would like to make in Korean family life. Tell what you would expect to accomplish by each of them.

16. What obstacles would you expect to meet in persuading the average Korean to accept these changes?

17.* What new moral ideals would be needed in order to make these changes effective?

18. Why are these ideals especially needed in the present crisis?

19. How can these ideals be secured?

20. Tell how you would present Christianity to meet the needs of Korean society.

21. Give passages of Scripture that you think would be most useful.

REFERENCES FOR FURTHER STUDY
CHAPTER IV

I. *Korean Character.*

Gale: Korean Sketches, chs. II, IX, X, pp. 23, 238-243.

Gifford: Every-day Life in Korea, pp. 59, 66-69.

Hulbert: The Passing of Korea, ch. II.

Bishop: Korea and Her Neighbors, pp. 235, 236, 336, 337.

Underwood: The Call of Korea, pp. 44-51.

Underwood: Fifteen Years Among the Topknots, pp. 273-276.

II. *The Position of Woman.*

Hulbert: The Passing of Korea, ch. XXVIII.

Bishop: Korea and Her Neighbors, pp. 114-120, 339-343, 355.

Gifford: Every-day Life in Korea, pp. 59-63.

Underwood: The Call of Korea, pp. 52-55, 61-63.

Noble: Ewa: A Tale of Korea, ch. II.

SPECIAL PROVIDENCES

SPECIAL PROVIDENCES

A second cause contributing to the success of missionary work in Korea is found in the conditions amidst which the missionaries labored. Misgovernment and oppression had reduced the people to despair. The measures taken for commercial and political betterment under native leadership had terminated in disappointing failure. The people were tired out, weary, and disheartened with the barrenness of pagan beliefs and religions. Morally they were decrepit and moribund. Into the gloomy, chilly atmosphere of their moral life came the gospel of Jesus Christ with its radiant promises of better things, and the Koreans turned as instinctively to it as the flower to the sunshine. There has been a lack of competition with Christianity which has given to Christian forces virtually a monopoly of the field. No great educational development or commercial expansion, no large military and naval development has taken place to challenge and hold the attention of the people. There has not yet arisen in Korea a many-tongued press and literature, with its babel and clamor of beliefs and propositions to dispute with Christianity the control of the intellectual life of the people. The only new literature, and, with few exceptions, the only periodicals issued, came from Christian sources. Each political change and disturbance of the social order has accelerated the turning of the Koreans to the Christian Church, while the absence of a nationalistic idea has resulted in a lack of strength and virility in the devotion of the average Korean to his religious beliefs.

—*George Heber Jones*

V

SPECIAL PROVIDENCES

It is noticeable that missionaries who are long in the interior develop a kind of hermit instinct that makes them shun the company of their fellows. One dear wife, in her lonely exile, mourned for two years the loss of faces, voices, and companionships that had been her joy and had made the world for her; for the next two years she awoke to new environments and found her soul tuned to new vibrations; for all the years afterward she was out of touch forever with the world that she had wept over. Its voices were not agreeable, its faces foreign, and she was at home and at peace with the yellow world and all its yellow ways. There is a disease that might be called *hermitoid,* that manifests itself in a desire to be alone. Like malaria it will overtake the missionary unless he guards against it. Nations too may fall victims to the same complaint. The victims avoid all foreign invitations; they shun commerce; they mistrust everybody; they want

to be alone.   This was Korea's complaint, till
the decade of the eighties.

Former
Opposition to
Foreigners

The present universally beloved and honored
Director of Religious Work in the Young Men's
Christian Association, S. J. Yi, was secretary
to the first embassy to Japan in 1876.   It was
a great and unheard-of venture for Korea to
reach out as far as Kobe, she being the Hermit.
When there an Englishman sent in his card to
the ambassador and said, "Let us meet and be
friends."   The ambassador said, "Don't touch
it. Send it back and say, 'We have no dealings
with foreigners.' "   Sign-posts along the way
as late as 1880 said: "If you meet a foreigner,
kill him, he who has friendly relations with
him is a traitor to his country."   There seemingly is not a moment of quiet or a place of
privacy in the whole land, and yet the broad
base of Korea's soul has marked on it, "Let me
be alone."

Ignorance of the
World

Three great nations closed right in upon her,
but the walls held, and, until the eighties,
scarcely even the name of a foreign country
was known.   In 1889 the writer met the governor of Whanghai province, and in the course
of conversation learned that that dignitary did
not even know the name of America, *Mi-guk,*

or *Yöng-guk,* England, but thought that the Western world was all one country, *Yang-guk.* He knew of China as the Great Country, *Tă-guk,* and of Japan as *Wă-guk,* Contemptible Dwarf Land. His world was still flat, and in the middle of it all was China, while on the east side of it was Korea. If you went far enough there were falling-off places into nowhere. All outside races were barbarians, and Korea desired converse with none of them.

While other parts of the Orient were touched by this and that influence, Korea as though by order of some great resident-general was kept closely locked and barred. When the Chinese envoy came bringing a message from the Yellow Emperor, he had a long train of retainers and hangers-on, horses and camels following. It would seem as though Korea would be occupied permanently by this invading army, but not so, for when the envoy retired all others were "shooed" out after him. "Go in peace but go," was the parting word. The retired scholar in the hills, living in a little hut, who sits with rod and line by the side of a stream catching no fish, but ever dreaming endless dreams of three thousand years ago, this man was the ideal of old Korea, the Hermit, the *Unsa.*

Unreached by Outside Influences

Suddenly the command was issued from somewhere, "Open wide the gates," and lo, in stepped the missionary. The doors had remained fast closed till he was ready, but now the hour had come. From that day on the missionary has been the representative Westerner, not the merchantman nor the official, but the missionary, the *moksa,* pacing the length and breadth of the land, in the far north, down south, all the way from Seoul to Fusan, to Wi ju, gazed at by wondering multitudes.

Korea might have remained a hermit still, had not a great war brought her prominently before the world. The greatest armies of modern times have marched across Korea; fleets that would eclipse the Armada have steamed round her shores. The greatest naval battle that the world ever saw took place within sound of her coast-line. God was pushing out the recently discovered Hermit to catch the attention of the world. The battle of the Yalu (Korea's northern border line) between Kuroki and the Russians really opened the war, and the fleet that steamed out of Masanpo (south port of Korea) really closed it. Included within the limits of the war were not only her boundaries, but her fate, her future.

GROUP OF PRESBYTERIAN MISSIONARIES ITINERATING

ITINERATING

Not only was she pushed before the world by newspaper reporters, war correspondents, and political writers, but the Hidden Hand linked her to the world's newest and greatest highway. In place of being a forgotten corner, she is now a part of the steel rings that encircle the earth. To this once unvisited city of Seoul, callers are coming from all over the world. Sunday after Sunday we have visitors who look down on the congregation from the platform, visitors from Japan, America, China, India, Europe, Australia. Korea is not modern like Japan, she is older than China, and yet here is the West, sitting by and looking on. God is using Korea as a missionary advertising agency for the whole Far East, and the line of callers is unbroken and growing in breadth and thickness. "How wonderful," they say, "to see these hundreds of people gathered here in worship!" "What are they talking about?" "He shall make you free, free from self, free from sorrow, free from sin, free from sickness and death," and they all sing "Hallelujah." The sightseer says that this is wonderful and passes on to tell of the awakening in the Far East. Korea is evidently being used as a pivot-point for the whole hemisphere.

So Small

It is fitting that Korea should play a special part in the progress of missions, for Korea is small as compared with adjoining territory and population. It has only 80,000 square miles. Shan-tung alone has 53,762, and a population of 36,247,000, a little more than half the size, with three times the population. The attention called to Korea these days seems by some special ordinance; for, man to man, it is far out of proportion to its size and population. A little, old remnant of a people seems about all they are as compared with the teeming multitudes of China, the dusty-coated hordes of Russia, or the picturesquely advertised world of Japan. Assuredly the last is first.

Self-government and Self-defense

Neither the science of self-government nor the science of self-defense is known to this people. They have got along with government under despots for generations past, and have been protected by no one knows whom, till at last a wild realization has settled over them that they have no king and no defense. Is this not one of the terrible facts that must confront one ere we see Jesus in all his attributes to save? We must conclude, after the surprises and changes of the last twelve years, that man's hand is not in it, that cabinets and governments

are outside of it, and that God has brought this
last, little, long-forgotten people to the place
where they say, "We have no king and no defense." His reply out of the thick clouds of
sorrow is, "Behold my Son, he is your King,
and he is your Defense."

The place that trouble holds in the world of **Trouble**
Christian experience, the turbulent seas of Galilee, the prisons, the lions' dens that await the
Christian on his pilgrimage, are of intense interest to the Korean. He studies them; he
thinks of Peter under iron gate and guard, of
Paul and Silas with feet in the stocks, of John
on Patmos, and he comes to the absurd conclusion that these men are not really Roman
prisoners, but rulers of the world. Then he
says: "Here am I; nobody knows the trouble I
see; my nation is shipwrecked; we are all in
prison." A son who was a political suspect
wrote to his father from the lock-up, "I'm in
prison." The father answered, "Be patient,
my son, we are all in prison." "Among tigers"
is a fruitful theme for story-writers and political speakers; the Christian, however, with
vision cleared for the distant horizons, sings,
"Stand up my soul, shake off thy fears."
Wedded to God's good news is tribulation.

How absurd it seems, and yet it is certainly so in the days of our best experience. They have met in Korea, these two, and hand in hand they move persuasively everywhere, into the Palace, into the hut back of the grinding-mill, into the schoolroom, into the life of the lost, into the den of the slave, till trouble becomes a beautifully arched bridgeway to the regions of freedom and joy. As Cæsar, the great enemy of the Jew, ruled at the time when the Savior himself came to visit them, so to-day under the rod of the alien a universal gospel invitation goes forth.

Korea's Position   Three great nations press close up around Korea. Japan to the fore, a first-rate power, is in command. She rules, keyed up to concert pitch. Very little remains for her for further advance; all the taxes she can bear, all the army she can raise, all the navy she can stand, this is Japan. No marked change in her near future is expected or is possible. Korea is perfectly helpless in her hands, and if no other consideration were involved in the question of the Far East, her place would be fixed world without end. But Korea's place and Korea's future are by no means settled. To the north and west are the world's greatest questions as to nations, Russia and China.   Russia, half awake, elbows the East all along its northern boundary, Persia, Mongolia, China, Korea, Japan.   Everybody is aware of Russia, and reports concerning the White Czar pass constantly.   Korea spells it "white" and "king", "white" up above and "king" down below and that spells a special character meaning "supreme emperor."   White Czar points fatefully to the ultimate supremacy of the Russias in the East.

On the west is China, snoring soundly as from a sleep of opium.   Will she awake some day, colossus of the world?   We love her.   The Chinaman somehow stands for diligence, simplicity, capability, good order, mind-your-own-business, indifference, geniality, superstition, lack of hygiene, trustworthiness.   Heaped up against Korea's west boundary line are his uncountable millions.   There was something exceedingly impressive in the quiet voice of Hudson Taylor when he said "China's millions."   What possible relation has the atom to the mass? and yet God has put Korea here and surrounded her by these portentous possibilities.   Undoubtedly her position has in it something of God's great plan.   Let the stu-

China's Millions
on the West

dent of missions ponder well over the map of
Asia and see where and how Korea sits.

Language

We think we see a providence in the matter
of Korea's written and spoken languages. Being a little country she has but one speech, and
when a man of the north says, "Peace," to the
man of Quelpart, he understands and answers
"Pyung-an-hassio" (Peace). Their ears are
all tuned to the same sounds, though there are
variations of dialect, as between the Scotch and
Irish, each of whom understands the other
perfectly and each maintains that his talk is the
standard "King's English".

Three Written Forms

As for written languages she has no less
than three: pure Chinese, pure *Un-mun,* and
mixed script. Japan, while somewhat similarly
situated to Korea in the matter of language,
has not all her freedom. Poor China flounders
about hopelessly trying to find some vehicle
that will convey thought from the page to the
mind of the simple. She tries the character and
labors hard to learn it. The teacher, in ex-
plaining the ideograph to the pupil, says: "Now
listen. When you have 'heart' to left and
'blood' to right, the character means 'to
pity'; but when you have 'heart' on one side
and 'star' on the other, it means 'wake up'.

When there is 'hand' on one side, and 'foot' on the other, it means 'to take hold'. When 'water' is on one side, and 'stand up' on the other, it means 'to cry'. When it has two 'speeches', and 'sheep' standing between them, it means 'good'. When 'grass' is on top and 'name' is down below, it means 'tea', and so on and so on, till the brain grows dizzy, and two thousand characters and more are learned. Then they must be read from the string along which they are strung. "For-father-thing-do-one-son-also-do-father-love-son-so-already-everything-do-one-make-know." This represents the struggle of China, Korea, and Japan after thought through the medium of the character. How labored and shadowy, but how simple when run out in native script: "For the thing the Father does, the Son does also; the Father loves the Son, and shows him all he does."

Korea's native script is surely the simplest language in the world. Invented in 1445 A. D., it has come quietly down the dusty ages, waiting for, who knew what? Never used, it was looked on with contempt as being so easy. Why yes, even women could learn it in a month or little more; of what use could such a cheap

Un-mun, or the Native Script

script be? By one of those mysterious providences it was made ready and kept waiting for
the New Testament and other Christian literature. Up to this day these have had almost
exclusive use of this wonderfully simple language. This perhaps is the most remarkable
providence of all, this language sleeping its
long sleep of four hundred years, waiting till
the hour should strike on the clock, that it
might rise and tell of all Christ's wondrous
works. They call it Un-mun, the "dirty language," because it is so simple and easy as
compared with proud Chinese picture writing.
God surely loves the humble things of life, and
chooses the things that are naught to bring to
naught the things that are. Tied in the belts
of the women are New Testaments in common
Korean; in the pack of the mountaineer on
his brisk journeying; in the wall-box of the
hamlet home; piled up on the shelf of the living-room are these books in Un-mun telling
of *Yesu* (Jesus), mighty to save. The writer
counts it among his choicest privileges that he
has had a share in its translation, that to him
were assigned John, Acts, Romans, Galatians,
Ephesians, and Revelation.

Mixed Script   As for the third language we have the mixed script. It is composed partly of Chinese characters and partly of pure Un-mun, and is used by Chinese readers and those who are fairly well educated. The Korean might be said to be three quarters eye and one quarter ear. He is never sure of a sentence till he sees it. You may say, "Sit still now till I read it to you. Yes, I'll even spell it out to you." He'll repeat it after you, and yet he is not sure of the meaning till he sees it. When he sees it, he exclaims, "Oh, now I understand." When he reads Chinese out loud he does not do so for the benefit of listeners, nor does he do so that his own ears may hear, he repeats the sound in order that his eye may be helped to see more clearly. The place of the eye, and the relative importance of sight as compared with hearing is a very interesting subject to students of the East.

The result is that we have three written languages, and a vast army of readers. Whereas in China and India one among a thousand perhaps can read, in Korea reading is almost universal. Those who have had no education can in a month or so "awake" to the common script, and are possessors of the Bible. Is it not a sign and a wonder that in this old forgotten land, with its conservative notions and

A Vast Army of Readers

backward ways, the New Testament should be sold by millions of portions and whole copies?

Another providence is that they have been preserved a literary people through all the changes of the past. They are not commercial nor military, but are literary. They exalt books, and so the Book of all books is gladly welcomed. They honor high teachings, and the gospel is treated as a prince bearing his tribute of righteousness, peace, and joy. This being the case, the missionary has had prepared for him a special place of honor, prepared from past ages and awaiting his arrival. He is the man with the book, not the man who comes to deal in lands, houses, or money; he is a spiritual master of literature, a teacher, a guide, a model for the common man. How shall we express regret sufficient for the missionary who fails to hold the exalted place prepared for him and given by this people?

The fact that education has been the supreme object or prize of Korean ambition evidences another special providence. More than for wealth or office, he has longed for scholarship. To be a litterateur and able to read the dots and strokes and spear-points of the Chinese character was the all in all of existence. The scholar was a king, and associated with him were the dragon, the phenix, the unicorn, the tortoise, and the stork—all of these having to do with profound spiritual meaning's. These attainments cut him off from the common haunts of men as the mountain forest is cut off and stands alone, hence he is called *Sa-rim* (Teacher Woods), or *San-lim* (Mountains and Woods), or *Yu-rim* (Confucian Forest), or *Eun-il* (Run Away and Hide).

His was a long and arduous course of study, and if we measure attainment by hours consumed, by feats of memory, by the manipulation of most difficult signs, certainly the degree of a Korean scholar meant more than one from Yale, Oxford, or Johns Hopkins.

Long and Arduous Course of Study

He begins by reading the *Thousand Character Classic,* then the *Tong-mong Son-seup* (The Primer), a book which deals with the Five Principles. Then several Chinese histories are read, the student never learning anything about his own country, but of China only —Mencius, the *Analects,* the *Doctrine of the Mean,* the *Books of History and Poetry,* and finally the *Yi-king,*—king of all absurd compositions. For a third of the time the student reads, for a third of the time he composes, for

Curriculum and Results Produced

a third of the time he writes. From twenty
years of this treadmill comes forth a peculiar
but most interesting type of graduate. From
long contact with imperious and opinionated
teachers, he has grown perfect in the matter of
respect to seniors, his downsittings and upris-
ings are all in accordance with eternal law, his
manner of deportment would delight a czar or
imperial Mogul, his powers of concentration
and attention are remarkable, his refinement of
bearing most distinguished, and in forms of
expression and dignity he could teach a prince.
Within certain fixed limits he is a poet, a prose
writer, a dreamer, a dream. It seems like sacri-
lege to break into this old and interesting
world, but, like Burns to the daisy, there is no
help for it:

> "Stern Ruin's plowshare drives, elate,
>   Full on thy bloom,
>   Till crushed beneath the furrow's weight
>   Shall be thy doom."

The Present

The new century with keen colter and long
share has driven, is driving, will drive, through
all the ideals of the East, and with them education. The rooms that once echoed with the
voices of little boys shouting out the old
phrases, as they memorized the *Thousand*

BEGINNING OF A SCHOOL FOR GIRLS

KOREAN TEACHER WITH PUPILS

Character Classic, are silent, and instead, on benches arranged in rows, sit a new generation of this new century learning arithmetic, geography, history, and the other branches of modern education. The change is the most momentous that has come in a thousand years; namely, that the ideals and gods of yesterday should to-day be dishonored and forgotten. Some of us have seen it with our eyes, have lived through this revolution, have lived in it over a span of twenty centuries, out of yesterday's B. C. into to-day's A. D. Is it a dream or is it real? Are these people those of twenty years ago, with their thoughts and desires and purposes, or are they another race who have been grafted on in a night, and have I slept like Rip Van Winkle and lost track of my bearings?

Christian schools are the crying need. To **Mission Schools** catch this wave on the crest and this moment ere it pass is our heart's desire for Korea. In Ping yang and Seoul already schools have been established where the students make as good a showing as in any place in the world, though they say the multiplication table backwards and write the denominator of a fraction before they write the numerator.

Desire for
Education

A great fever for education has taken possession of the people of the peninsula. At every public gathering where education is mentioned, it touches a thousand electric buttons, and men are on their feet, wide awake, and excitement runs high. All eyes are bright when education speaks. Schools are cropping out of the soil like mushrooms. Tight-fisted men who never gave a cash for the welfare of another are aroused by the call for education to advance thousands. Names are widely advertised to-day, such as The Wake-up School, The School of Great Achievement, Forward March School, The College of Fair Letters, and similar designations.

Right
Adjustment to
the State

The government is trying to find some way to handle the educational question and keep it from running away with the state; a set of rules and regulations has just been issued by which all the odds and ends and little facts and great shall be known about all the schools in all the land, whether the School of Great Achievement or the College of Fair Letters.

Books and Other
Developments

This wild thirst for knowledge has never been seen before, was unheard of till the present day; now it is realized, and the thirsty man will drink. Books are pouring out of the

presses, such as *Kyung-kuk Mi-tam,* which tells
the immortal story of Athens and Sparta; one
about Madame Roland, one about Garfield, one
on Garibaldi, one on the time of King John of
England, on Algebra, Trigonometry, Meta-
physics, Surveying and many other subjects.
Groups of young men are seen going about
with light red-ringed poles and tables for re-
cording every angle and measuring every hill.
The difference in time represented by a map of
the city made ten years ago and one made to-
day by these young surveyors is the difference
between the days of Balaam the prophet and
Edison the seer.

One young man, an earnest Christian, and
altogether a gentleman, has the name of being
the best teacher of mathematics in the city. He
is worn down by the incessant calls on his time.
He teaches an hour here and then dashes off in
his jinrickisha to teach an hour yonder. On into
the night he keeps up this treadmill till his face
is pale and his body worn down by the grind
of it.   Hundreds of young men are after him
like hounds on the scent.   Fathers who yesterday whiffed the pipe of indifference and rumi-
nated of Yo and Sun, are but ghosts and shades
compared with these sons and daughters of

New Currents
of Interest

theirs who care not a rap for the Yellow Emperor of China, 2300 B. C., but want to know why x minus y multiplied by x plus y equals x square minus y square.

A Revolution

This is not the French Revolution and there is no Feast of Pikes, but a revolution it is, and a kicking off of old shackles and feet-clamps and such a breaking of rusted links as the East never saw before. What will the end be? It will be that this old picturesque corner of the world will become prosaic West, and the subject thereof will be a good or bad man according as he meets with the good or bad to lead the way.

Public Utilities

Already we have electric cars running the length of the city, managed by Koreans, and they make first-class motormen; a line of steel rails stretches the length of the peninsula and couples it on to Europe and the Western world. Hydrants all along Bell Street bubble with water from the river five miles away, pure and safe, compared with the pestiferous wells from which the people of the city formerly drank. Young men of to-day talk of hygiene and microbes and bacteria, so that the old conservative who does not believe a word of it sees his world drifting from beneath his feet.

In a most providential and wonderful way, Korea has been preserved as a sort of model of Bible times and Bible lands. In the early days of missionary experience so many of these associations crossed one's path that we walked as in a dream; later, familiarity somewhat dulled the consciousness of them, and they are forgotten or overlooked, but even yet after twenty years, notwithstanding all the changes that have occurred, voices and scenes call up the days of David and Daniel, Peter and Paul.

A Model of Scripture Times

When a man bows down, low down, or worships before God, his face is literally in the dust, and his brow touches the ground. Thus David bowed before Saul[1], and thus Saul bowed before the ghost of Samuel[2]. All about us are salutations of "Peace", "Peace", "Go in peace", "Sleep in peace", "Eat in peace", "Rest in peace", *"Pyung-an, Pyung-an",* as the old Hebrews said "Shalom" or the Moslems still to-day say "Salaam". It calls up the Savior's words in John xiv. 27. It was the salutation in his time; it is the salutation in Korea to-day. When the native reads the Bible it speaks of peace to him, and it speaks it in a much more

Salutations

---

[1] 1 Sam. xxiv. 8.

[2] 1 Sam. xxviii. 14.

intelligible way than it does to the American or European.

References to
Marriage and
Other Customs

"Behold, the bridegroom! Come ye forth to meet him." Here he comes mounted high on his white charger, with royal robes on, accompanied by an army of glad retainers who shout, "Clear the way, the bridegroom cometh." How much it seems like dreamland. All untouched by the rest of the world, these customs have held till Jesus came, and thus his words and his times are most familiar; thus too the watches of the night, and the cockcrow of the morning.

The Law of
Sacrifice

The great law of sacrifice, so dimly understood by Western people, is the commonest talk of Korea. For thousands of years sheep and oxen have died for the sins of the people. Birds and beasts have been offered in a vain effort to lift this burden from the human soul. I read in a history of Korea that in the year when our Savior was born in Bethlehem, the king of Kokuryu went out into the open plain to offer sacrifice to God. Two 'swine beasts' were to be offered, but in the preparation of the sacrifice they took to their heels and ran away. The king sent two officers in pursuit, Messrs. Takni and Sappi. They chased the pigs to Long Jade

Lake, caught them and hamstrung them, so that they could not run again; then they dragged them before the king. "How dare you", said he, "offer to God a mutilated sacrifice?" He had these two gentlemen buried alive for their sin, but behold he himself shortly after fell seriously ill. A spirit medium called and told him his sickness was due to the sin of having killed Takni and Sappi. He confessed, and prayed, and was cured of his complaint.

In this story old as our era, we read of the need of a sacrifice to God, of a perfect sacrifice, of sin being followed by punishment, of forgiveness following confession. A race drilled in stories like this find no difficulty in the great vicarious sufferings of Jesus. His perfect offering is simplicity itself; his forgiveness of sin the logical outcome of his whole attitude of heart.

Ideas Long Prevalent

The expression, "Girt about the breasts with a golden girdle,"[1] is never quite clear to a young Bible reader at home, and China and Japan cast no special light upon it; but in Korea there was the long white robe down to the feet, and round the breast the embroidered girdle. It remained until after the missionary arrived,

References to Dress

---

[1] Rev. i. 13.

and then in the changes of the new century the girdle was swept away. The white robes too find their corresponding part in Scripture, and the expression, "So as no fuller on earth can whiten them,"[1] often came to mind in the old days, when out of the little squalid huts came forth coats that shone like polished marble.

Foot-gear

Then there is the foot-gear or sandals. Neither China nor Japan so markedly reflects Scripture in this respect as Korea. Here are the strings tied over the instep, here the humble servant is called to bow down and unloose them. As in Judea, they are never worn indoors but are dropped off on the entrance-mat.

The Bed

"Take up thy bed, and walk,"[2] seemed to the writer in his boyhood days as a most extraordinary expression. He pictured a four-posted bed being tugged out of a bedroom by one poor man only just recovered of his sickness; but when he came to Korea, he understood it all. The bed was just a little mattress spread out on the floor of the living-room, and to roll it up and put it away was the common act of every morning when the sleeper awoke. Morning light and consciousness had come into

[1] Mark ix. 3.
[2] Mark ii. 9, 10.

the life of the poor invalid, so he would roll
up his sleeping-mat and walk off to where it
was put for the day. In so many of the common acts of life in Korea we were in touch with
the days of our Lord on earth.

Especially are Koreans inquisitive and curi-
ous as to custom. Had the Scriptures been
filled with Western ways of life, it would have
taken all day and all these years to tell what
this and that meant; but, as they talk from
first to last about Korea's own world and own
people, there are few or no questions as to
custom.

Forestalls a Multitude of Questions

How far away the Bible seems to us when
it tells of sackcloth and ashes, and about Jacob[1]
and Mordecai[2] and Isaiah[3] who marked their
desolation by these signs. In Korea sackcloth
is still such a mark, and with hair unbound and
their persons wrapped about with these coarse
folds of bagging, they sit like Job and cry
"*Aigo, aigo.*" "And the mourners go about
the streets." From the writer's house we look
out on one of the main thoroughfares of the
city; and frequently, as the sun goes down,
there comes a procession bearing lanterns and a
long line of mourners in sackcloth following

Sackcloth and Ashes

[1] Gen. xxxvii. 34.   [2] Esther iv. 7.   [3] Isa. lviii. 5.

the dead with mournful wailings. Is there not a thought and a providence underlying the oneness of these things with all the settings of the Scripture?

Idolatry

What grinning teeth and glaring eyes meet you on the highways and byways of Korea that you unconsciously associate with Dagon, Moloch, Chemosh, and Baal, and other gods and idols to whom Israel bowed down. America has heard of idols, has seen them in museums, has looked on them through the pages of Scripture, but to see an idol actually in command of his own and at work would be thought almost an impossibility.

Demon Possession

Another fact that brings the people closely into touch with Christian thought is their understanding of demon possession. They accept it as a something not to be questioned any more than their own existence; demons are everywhere, and the casting of them out a lucrative profession. "By thy name cast out demons;"[1] "He cast out the spirits with a word;"[2] "Authority to cast out demons;"[3] "Mary Magdalene, from whom he had cast seven demons."[4] We of the West read these statements as if they belonged to another

[1] Matt. vii. 22. [2] Matt. viii. 16. [3] Mark iii. 15. [4] Mark xvi. 9.

planet. We question the whole subject of demon possession. Can it not be diagnosed by the doctors? Will not a tablet or a pill settle the matter? Is it not the misunderstanding of an unenlightened age? All of these questions put us so much out of touch with the story. The Korean's doubts are along another line. Can Jesus really cast them out? That's the question. Big devils as well and wicked? Is this all true, and does he care for the possessed and the imprisoned? "The devil we know and demon possession we are sure of, but just who is Jesus?" Surely the Korean's preparatory course has been eminently one to fit him for the reading and appreciating of the New Testament.

He attributes sickness in so many cases to **Sickness** the influence of malignant spirits. "Divers diseases,"[1] is a phrase terribly applicable to the filth, poverty, and teeming multitudes of the East. The twisted limbs, the blinded eyes, the diseased and marred bodies, were all invited, yes, and are all invited to come to Jesus, and according to your faith it shall be unto you. Assuredly God can take the wrath, the meanness, the sores, the impurity, the leprous spots,

---

[1] Matt. iv. 24; Mark i. 34; Luke iv. 40

of men and make them servants to minister to
his honor and glory.

A Gentleman

The representative Korean is a man something like Nicodemus, a gentleman by instinct,
habit, and manner of speech. He came by night
to see Jesus, afraid that he would lose "face" by
coming in the daytime. Korean-like, he begins
by a high expression of regard, "Teacher come
from God"; by a honorific, he knows Jesus is
true; he wants to follow him, his heart is prepared for the seed that falls, and eventually he
comes in at a critical moment for a service of
high honor. May it be with Korea as it was
at last with Nicodemus, a place of special consecration at the close of this gospel age! The
gentleness of this people, their appreciation of
high morals, notwithstanding the lack of the
same in their own history, their exalting of
principles of right, is a preparation for the
gospel call.

**Points Making
Koreans
Receptive**

Outwardly, by habit, custom, and ceremonial
form, they are equipped to understand the
Bible; the air they breathe seems impregnated
with the flavor of the days of Christ; the movings of their world are along the lines of
ancient Palestine; their inner thoughts are recorded in the Scriptures; their superstitions

just as they were in the days of Israel's decline; their understanding of spiritual forces just what the nations round Judea understood them to be; their conclusions concerning life what the worldly of the Bible concluded life to be.

To meet these conditions, is this wonderful language, Un-mun. Like the shot that hit the target, it strikes squarely into the opportunity of to-day, and prepares the land for what God is asking of it. Nationally last, least, and less than nothing, how beautifully is Korea suited to God's hand! At just this time, too, missionary boards are awake, and new forces are pressing in. Yesterday Korea sat weeping over her disbanded soldiers, to-day she welcomes the army of salvation to take the vacated and desolated place. Through these things a multitude of providences seem to shine and shimmer forth.

Providential Encouragements

SUGGESTIVE QUESTIONS ON CHAPTER V

Aim: To Understand the Providential Encouragements to Missionary Work in Korea

I. *The Providences of History and Geography.*

   1. State as vividly as you can the contrast between the exclusiveness of Korea thirty years ago and the situation to-day.

2. How completely has God answered the prayers that the doors of Korea might be opened?

3. What has he done to call the country into public prominence?

4. Why must it inevitably remain in public prominence?

5. Of what advantage has it been that the most representative foreigner has been the missionary?

6. Why does the size of Korea fit it for becoming a missionary object-lesson to the Far East?

7. Could you choose a more favorable geographical position for such an object-lesson?

8.* Why has Christianity a better chance to ally itself with Korean than with Chinese or Japanese patriotism?

9.* Sum up the message of Christianity to a people in political distress.

II. *The Providences of Language and Literature.*

10. Name several advantages to missionary work arising from the currency of a single spoken language throughout an entire country.

11. What would be the disadvantages to a nation of knowing only the Roman numeral system?

12. Would this be such an obstacle to progress as having only the Chinese character for literary purposes?

13.* What are the advantages to Christianity of having so promptly appropriated the Unmun script?

14. As far as literature is concerned, what would be the relative difficulty of evangelizing Korea and a province of China of the same size and population?

15. What practical effect should the Korean respect for literature have upon the training and methods of missionaries?

16.* What advantages has the missionary in Korea over the average African missionary in his evangelistic work?

17.* In view of present providences, make as strong an appeal as you can for evangelistic, literary, and educational missionaries for Korea to-day.

18. What practical recommendations would you make to the Church at home as to the support of educational institutions in Korea?

19. In what ways is the present a greater opportunity for education than either the past or the future?

20. How would you translate, "Behold the Lamb of God," for a people that had no sheep and no sacrifices?

21. In what ways would it be more difficult to translate the Bible into Esquimo than into Korean?

22.* Arrange the principal providences of missionary work in Korea in what seems to you the order of their importance.

REFERENCES FOR FURTHER STUDY
CHAPTER V

I. *Korean Education.*

Hulbert: The Passing of Korea, ch. XXVI.

Gifford: Every-day Life in Korea, ch. XIII (up to 1896).

Bishop: Korea and Her Neighbors, pp. 387-391.

Underwood: Fifteen Years Among the Topknots, pp. 303, 304.

PIONEER METHODS OF THE
MISSIONARIES

The missionary body in Korea is made up of a very superior company of men and women. Both sexes are apt to be college graduates, while the men are in addition graduates of seminaries or medical schools. Quite a number have shown marked scholarship in the study of the language, in interpretation and translation, and in general literature. Historical and descriptive works of value have been published by them, while at least one extended and well-received romance is the result of one man's leisure, and another was a contributor to some of our best magazines.

—*Horace N. Allen*

In the spring of 1890, Dr. and Mrs. Nevius, of Cheefoo, China, visited Seoul, and in several conferences laid before the missionaries there the method of mission work commonly known as the Nevius method. After careful and prayerful consideration, we were led, in the main, to adopt this, and it has been the policy of the mission first, to let each man "abide in the calling wherein he was found," teaching that each was to be an individual worker for Christ, and to live Christ in his own neighborhood, supporting himself by his trade.

Secondly, to develop Church methods and machinery only as far as the native Church was able to take care of and manage the same.

Third, as far as the Church itself was able to provide the men and the means, to set aside those who seemed the better qualified, to do evangelistic work among their neighbors.

Fourth, to let the natives provide their own church buildings, which were to be native in architecture, and of such style as the local church could afford to put up.

—*Horace G. Underwood*

VI

PIONEER METHODS OF THE
MISSIONARIES

On April 5, 1885, H. G. Underwood, the First Entrance
first clerical missionary, landed in Korea. Already
the Roman Catholics had been in the
country for forty-eight years; already a New
Testament had been printed in the native script
by John Ross of Mukden; already Chinese
books had reached the peninsula; already
many rumors of the Christian and the Christian's God had crossed the northern border.

Many priests of the Roman Catholic Church, Persecution
native, Chinese, and foreign, had been tortured
and put to death, and there was a fear associated with the foreign religion. Natives
still pointed out the place by the Han River
where Bishop Berneux and eight priests had
been beheaded. Jesus and Mary were names
with which to stop the heart-beat. One old
dame who had seen it all, and had outlived the
reign of terror, in telling it to the writer forty
years afterward, would not speak above her
breath. I asked: "Is your heart at peace?"

She replied "Whist, Yesu-Maria, my sons were in it you know, Yesu-Maria, Yesu-Maria." Although there has grown up, little by little, a distinction between *Yesu Kyo* (Protestantism) and *C'hun-ju Kyo* (Catholicism) it was not recognized at first, and the dread associated with the one gathered about the other.

Foreigners

Western people too, as well as their doctrines, were unsavory. There had been an American ship captured and its crew massacred in Ping yang, in 1866. In the same year a French expedition was fitted out against Kanghwa. In 1871, Americans had come in many ships and fought likewise. In 1875, the Japanese came and fought too, so that the West and the Japanese were alike. Kanghwa the island at the mouth of the Han River. has been a broad target for all shots, from the days of Kublai Khan (1225) to Admiral Rodgers and Commodore Shufeldt (1867, 1871, 1883).

The Pioneers

Fortunately the missionary entered Korea with many things arrayed against him. Had everything been in his favor, his work would have been easy and very badly done, but he had to fight every inch of the way. Let the reader think what he would do first, if he were asked to transport America over to the East

piecemeal, where would he begin, what would
he ship first, and when would he expect to get
through? About as bewildering a problem is
it to carry the gospel to an entirely new race
and new people, having to place before each
person, little by little, our motives, our expec-
tations, our customs, our hearts especially,
ere we can get into tune to begin Bible work
and Scripture teaching. Let us be thankful
that the pioneers were just the right men for
the work on hand. While the Hon. H. N.
Allen, M. D., as a medical missionary opened
the work, in the mind of the writer he is dis-
associated from the missionary list. He was
a diplomatist, from his first entry till the close
of his distinguished career, in 1905. His name
stands high in Korea, honored and beloved by
native as well as foreigner, for he served many
years in behalf of Americans and this people
faithfully and well.

But of missionaries proper, Underwood and Qualities
Appenzeller were the clerical, and Heron and   Needed
Scranton the medical. It needed men of cour-
age, men of vision, men of courtly manner,
men of magnetism; it needed also men of
strong conviction and physical endurance, and
we had such qualifications in these four. Of

the Presbyterians, the writer recalls a day in 1888, his first tiffin in Seoul. Ten were at the table, among them these two pioneers. To-day after a score of years, he is alone on the field of all the ten. When he thinks back over that first bright company of the young hearts, each with life offered for Korea, of the hopes, of the vacant places now, of the long farewells, he would bow his head and repeat slowly:

"They climbed the steep ascent to heaven,
    Through peril, toil, and pain;
  O God! to us may grace be given
    To follow in their train."

Counter-
considerations

The considerations that have acted against the work have run somewhat as follows: For the first few years it was dangerous to be a Christian, it was counted the same as Roman Catholic, and Roman Catholics had been slaughtered by the thousands. Later it was not dangerous, but it was cheap, common; butchers, and basket-makers, and well-diggers, and shopkeepers, and coolies were all admitted; certainly it was no calling for a gentleman. Still later, in stirring political times, it was the popular thing to be a Christian, till it was discovered that the Church was "hands off" as regards Cæsar, that it was apathetic and no man with "sand" in his make up or "ginger" in his blood could afford to be a Christian. The converts seemed to sit by and see the country go to the dogs, so it was not for the patriot. Last of all the Church was not an enemy of Japan or the Japanese, therefore it was no good; it was neither for nor against, it was lukewarm, and the moving spirits of the land laughed it to scorn.

Still, in spite of opposition and seasons of great unpopularity, it forged ahead. God seems to love lines of greatest resistance, for only when forces are arrayed against him does his power show forth. Along these lines has it gone, till, gathered in one church meeting to-day, you can see princes, well-diggers, cabinet secretaries, butchers, merchants, distinguished literati, the poor, the rich, Joseph of Arimathæa, blind Bartimæus, educationalists, students, clerks of the law department, ex-governors, vice-ministers, and in short people of every condition and station. Into all classes of society has the gospel gone, and bearing down all opposition, carried with it proofs of its power to save. *Opposition Steadily Overcome*

In pioneer work there are, without question, *Hardships*

hardships, but there are also compensations great and wonderful. The writer can best illustrate what all other missionaries have passed through by telling a little of his own first experiences. What were the hardships? There are seven of them, complete and fully rounded out as to number.

Sitting on the Heated Stone Floor

First, should be mentioned sitting all day on the heated stone floor. You ask, "Why not use a chair?" Because it would be as much out of place as if a Korean should call on you and, instead of sitting on a chair, should sit on the floor and talk up at you. It would put you out of touch at once with the very world you were endeavoring to get at. Let the reader try sitting cross-kneed for three hours at a stretch, if he would fully understand this paragraph. To some it becomes a veritable torture-rack, knees and hip-joints and ankle bones are crying out against you. You rest this one and the others only scream the louder. There is nothing for it but a chair or to go out for a walk. Still the sitting life is a part of your calling, and in the early days it was absolutely necessary.

Sleeping on the Heated Floor

Second, the sleeping. For those of us who have slept for some years as the Koreans do,

on the hot floor, it was practise in the science
of being baked brown. On many a cold night
the floor seemed at first grateful, but as the
hours went by the room became a Dutch oven,
and you were being cooked. All night the
tossings and the tumblings would continue,
mixed with fire and labored dreamings, the
room stifled for want of ventilation, and the
whole universe apparently in torment.

Third, the food. Instead of fruit, cereals, **Food**
bacon and eggs, a cup of coffee, you would be
served with rice for breakfast, cabbage and
turnips in salt water, dried fish shredded, red
pepper soup, and other preparations, the odor
thereof being strong. Epicurean-like, your
whole being would long for a mutton-chop,
pancakes, hot biscuits, ice-cream, and other
favorite dishes, but in all the flavors of the
busy day not one of these was present.

Fourth, the crowds of men. How they **Crowds**
would trample over you! To quote from *The
Vanguard:* "On into the night his room was
the rendezvous for all classes. Men with Mon-
gol thoughts and fetid breath sat cross-kneed
about him, shouting all manner of useless questions over and over, proposing that he measure
his strength of arm with them, asking for his

hat and boots to try on." Frequently when
night came three or four of these callers would
stretch out on the floor of the seven by eight
by ten room to sleep, the hottest end of the
bake-oven being given to the foreigner as a
mark of honor. Every door was closed and no
chink of ventilation was allowed open lest
Horangee, the tiger, come and eat you. These
people were never unkind or impolite, but the
endless crowds of men wore one's soul down.
You never seemed to make any headway. A
new crowd would come, and all the old salutations and explanations would have to be gone
over. Never before did we realize what the
world would be without woman, no woman's
voice, no evidence of woman's hand, none of
the refinements of society that are seen only in
the world of emancipated women, but only
coarse-grown, greedy, sensual men, full of
pride and empty egotism.

Vermin

Fifth, vermin. Where Buddha has had a
hand and a hearing, there vermin exist and
are glad. Some are large enough to be seen,
some so small that you might mistake them for
nothing. Like the cholera *comma bacillus,* they
are not to be measured by a foot-rule, but it
seems to me that they are more terrible than

an army with banners and field-guns. It would
be quite improper to go into details of the fight.
Suffice it to say that during those early years
mountains of agony seemed to overwhelm one,
whereas the cause was but the merest trifle,
not large enough to put a pin through or fasten
onto the cardboard of a natural history
museum.

Sixth, sickness and death. The loathsome, **Sickness and**
fearsome nature of disease is never seen till you **Death**
go as a missionary to some benighted, idol-
beridden land. There you see sickness in all
its lurid colors. Just one example: I was to
take a meeting at a neighboring house, and the
master had come to show the way. He remarked, "We have 'pimples' at our house just
now, so the meeting will be all the better." Just
what kind of pimples possessed his house I
did question, but did not guess. When I arrived, the wife came out to greet me. All were
so glad that the *moksa* was to lead the meeting. Pimples! I should think so! There sat
the wife's brother at the doorway just covered
with smallpox pustules. My first impulse was
to go away, but on second thought that did not
seem satisfactory. God had brought me, I
must stay. We had the meeting. "Jesus walk-

ing on the water" was the subject. The patient would sometimes cry, and then again he would stifle his agony, brighten up, and listen. "Sit over there," said I, "there's a draft here where I am sitting." I was so thankful there was a draft.

Pagan and Christian Usage

Death, ever present all the world over, how softened his grim visage is when associated with the name of Jesus, how awful when he appears alone. The writer still recalls one summer long ago, May, 1889, when funeral preparations were being made before a neighboring house. He made inquiry of An, his host: "I didn't know that there was a death." "Yes, the master of the house is dead; they will bury him." "But when did he die? To-day when we were out?" "No, no, not to-day. He died before you came." I had been there two months. They had a bier ornamented with dragons' heads, painted in wild colors, that suggested skull and cross-bones. The funeral service was a fearful row, everybody was noisy, many were weeping, many were drunk. A more gruesome performance than that which I saw, over that horrible, unburied body, no one could imagine. To-day that same village sits as it did then, with background of mountain and foreground of sea, but how changed! All is Christian, Sunday is a day of rest, and every house is represented at the service in the chapel. They have lived down old-fashioned death in that village and exchanged it for quiet sleep.

Seventh, the language. This is a trial **The Language** harder than the reader can well imagine. In a sense you have to take the place of a child and prattle in monosyllables, and say foolish things, and make no end of silly mistakes, and cover all your friends with confusion, over and over. You may be wise, and think great thoughts, but in actual experience you are less than the least. This humiliation lasts for a year or so, sometimes it lasts longer, sometimes it lasts forever and a day. One often prays, "O for the day of Pentecost, when even the illiterate Peter could soar like the eagle over the nations of the world!" but it comes not in that way. It is best that we learn little by little, and by a very humble pathway, but it is a hardship indeed.

In missionary work, first and foremost, con- **First Secret in Missionary Work** fidence must be established and the heart won. The missionary may be learned, may be hard-working and godly, may be earnest as John Knox, and indefatigable as Mr. Moody, but if the people do not love him, they will not listen to his doctrine. It is a terrible fact that there are some missionaries on the field who are not loved by the people. While unlovely and unloved, all they do is as wood, hay, and stubble. As in wireless telegraphy there must be harmony of note between despatcher and receiver, so, ere messages to the soul pass, despatcher missionary and receiver Oriental must be in tune. What wonders you can do when the heart is won! The multitude may hold you in its grip, from dawn till sunset, still next day you are full of hope again. It is the missionary in tune with God and with the heart of the East who does the work. Let much emphasis be put on the right key as to the heart, for therein lies the secret.

Other Secrets

Every day come the crowds. What would the reader tell them first, these brand new hearers? "Jesus, who is he?" "How could God have a Son?" "The Bible? Who knows?" "Let's read," and little by little the work narrows itself down to reading together the New Testament. Here again is another secret of success. Argument is of no avail. Telling the whole story by the half hour together counts little; but to sit down, offer a prayer for God's light and leading, and then read, means the entrance of the Word. Another secret is to leave matters alone that you are not called upon to speak of. Read and pray. Get Jesus into the lost soul, and then ancestor worship and rags and kitchen devils and filth and ignorance will dissipate, like the darkness when the sun shines over Camel Mountain and lights up our hill in the morning. This has been the way of the cross in Korea, not by street preaching, not by great crowds, not by spectacular effort, but in the little room seven by seven by ten, seated cross-kneed on the matting, with the Bible opened and somebody to read and pray with.

Keeping time with the first stages of the work is the press. The toil and sweat and agony that accompanies the management of a Western printing plant in the Far Orient baffles description. There may be breaks, smashings, losings, pages with lines upside-down, but "Never mind," says the Orient, "Reverse the book and read it down the other way, the thought is all right." Gray hairs come out like snowbirds on a wintry day, and sit all round the superintendent's ears, but he too has to keep heart in tune, be one with his blundering men,

The Press

love them, and pray with them. That is the main part of the lesson.

In Korea from the day of Rev. F. Ohlinger's setting up the press till the present, when several large Japanese and Korean houses are established, what a work of grace has been done by this Methodist superintendent! No one can measure or calculate or guess in the least the extent to which his work has aided the proclamation of the gospel. Not only the New Testament and portions, like the Gospels, have gone out in thousands upon thousands, but tracts like "The Two Friends", "The Peep of Day", *Pilgrim's Progress,* and similar writings. The struggle to have the printed page keep pace with the proclamation and the loud demand have gone on for twenty years, and to-day (1908) bookmen come, saying, "We are out of books, what are we going to do?" A change however has come about. If the Tract Society now fails to keep up the supply, individual Christians publish the books themselves. Recently the writer was asked for the manuscript of *The Life of Martin Luther.* "We must have it," said this Christian friend, "and as the Tract Society is unable to publish it, I'll do so myself," and thither went the manuscript.

Along with pioneer missionary effort went the translation of the Scriptures; and what a huge undertaking it is no one knows who has not tried it. Sixty stories of a life insurance building in New York City is not as big an undertaking. It takes about ten years to do it. If we think of all the digging necessary as a foundation on which to work, of every shovelful of paragraphs, of what each word means, sifted and weighed and valued and recorded, with malaria and weariness all round about, it reminds one of digging the Panama Canal. A Panama Canal it is, this New Testament, linking two great oceans, the ocean of God's boundless love with the immeasurable expanse of human need.

When China was in the throes of Boxerdom, in 1900, we had just finished the New Testament, and some of the refugees were present when the Hon. H. N. Allen, M. D., United States minister, made a speech and presented specially bound copies to the translators.

Since then the Old Testament is under way and will in about a year more, we hope, be completed. Already Genesis, Exodus, Samuel, Kings, Psalms, Isaiah are on the market, and Koreans are reading about Joseph, Jonathan,

Elijah, and the wicked kings of Israel and Judah.

Use of Hymns

Wherever the gospel goes, hymns spring up, glad hymns, pathetic hymns, hymns that win the wayward and the wandering. Among those most in use in Korea are "Jesus loves me" (*"Yesu na-rul sa-rang hao"*), "Nothing but the blood" (*"P'i pak-keui up-nai"*), "Nearer, my God, to Thee" (*"Ha-na-nim kat-ka-hi"*), "Jerusalem, my happy home" (*"Ye-ru-sal-lem na pok toin chip"*). These are finding their way into huts that you have to bow down to crawl into, into high-class homes, into palaces, and the children are growing up with their vibrations in the air. The place that hymns have in the forward march of the gospel is worth noting, a place large and permanent. Thus far the foreign missionary has had much to do with the composition of Korean hymns, but later we shall have our Watts and Wesley, who will give us compositions that will stand like "Rock of Ages."

Bible Study Classes

The foreign missionary is, as we have seen, a starter and director of the work rather than the one who carries it out. Where his influence is seen to greatest advantage is in the classes for Bible study. These meet at various times

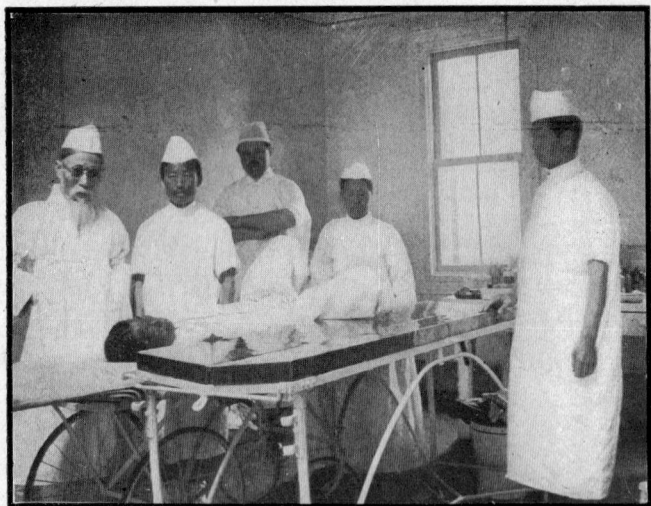

JUNKIN MEMORIAL HOSPITAL, FUSAN

IVEY HOSPITAL, SONGDO

during the year, the men at their suitable season and the women when it best suits them. For the two weeks or so that they are together these selected Christians are taught and helped in Bible study. They are full of questions as to the meaning of this and that in Gospels and Epistles, and the application of it to every-day life. While engaged in this work, they pray together, and enter into the business of it as men do into a joint-stock company of this world's affairs.

When the measure of mission work is taken for the wide mission fields of the world, many a medical man will come in for the wreath of laurel. In Korea this will be true. The first missionary to be appointed was a medical man, the first to arrive on the field was a medical man, the first great loss was a medical man. The medical missionary's life is a ceaseless war waged against typhus, and leprosy, and small-pox, and cholera, and all the fearsome heritage that has scourged humanity. His calling is to go into the most noisome dens of suffering, where poverty, crime, ignorance, and superstition sit huddled together, to go in with kindly expression and heart full of love for all mortals.

The Medical Missionary

An Ambassador
of Cause and
Effect

The question is sometimes asked as to just what place the medical missionary takes in the work of missions, and the answer is usually that he helps win the people. This is true, though it is also true that any one can win the people who loves them and is unselfish. But outside of this the medical worker has a distinct sphere of his own. He is the man who helps break down the ignorance and unreasonableness of non-christian nations. He is the ambassador of the law of cause and effect that the Orient has been out of touch with for all these ages. He teaches the first lessons in hygiene; he shows the difference between rags and royal robes; he is the representative of the advanced world of Christian thought, and no mission can afford to be without him.

Groundless
Oriental
Inferences

Even Chang Chih-tung, the distinguished man of China, only a few years ago attributed a cancerous formation on his face to a roadway that had been cut through an ancient hill near his home, and he straightway had it filled up. All down through Korean history we read how this and that phenomenon of nature was followed by this and that catastrophe in life. I read of 80 A. D. in the *Sam Guk Sa* (Korean History) : "In the fourth moon a great wind blew down the East Gate of the city, and in the eighth moon the king died." "Sure," says the old-time Eastern reader, just as we would when we read, "John Robinson Smith jumped from an express train, fell on his neck, and broke it."

The medical missionary turns his guns on this world and pounds its fortifications mightily. Yet he has to be patient withal, for perhaps while he is prescribing for the sick man the latest scientific output of a drug company, Grandma Kim, behind the house under the rear thatch, is brewing a decoction of deers' horns and ginseng to mix in, and when the man recovers "the deers' horns did it."

Medical Missionary has Need of Patience

The medical man fights dirt and filth, and in every direction we see them giving away and a new and cleaner order coming in. We may even have a shower of meteors these days without associating it with a plague of cholera or some other dire thing to follow.

Fights for Cleanliness

The medical man, too, falls like the soldier in the hot assault, and we comrades of his pass on over the way he has opened. Western medicine planted strongly in Seoul, in Syen chun, in Song chin, in Fusan, in Mokpo, takes in the center and four corners of the land. In-

Falls Like a Soldier

terspersed between, are eight hospitals or more
and dispensaries.

Graduates in Medicine

Last summer, at the Severance Hospital,
which is successor to the institution originally
founded by Drs. Allen and Heron and since
carried on by Avison and Hirst, seven students graduated in medicine and surgery.
Prince Ito was present to give the diplomas,
and the government granted them licenses to
practise as graduates in medicine. What an
advance since the days of the plaster of excre-
ment, or the long needle that was driven
through skin, flesh, muscles, veins, till it found
a bone to impinge upon and make the patient
see stars!

The Hospital

It is a joy to the clerical man to go through
the hospital and see these suffering sojourners
of the yellow Orient cared for by doctors,
nurses, and assistants who are wise enough
and good enough to wait on King Edward or
President Taft. The harelips that have been
sewed up, the stiff joints that have been set
free, the tumors that have been removed, the
bones that have been put right, the foul diseases that have been driven away, all speak for
the coming of the gospel.

Woman's Need

Among the most beneficent of all Christian

SEVERANCE HOSPITAL, SEOUL

efforts that of medical work for women surely
stands high. The woman's life, heretofore
weighted by all manner of oppression, and
impressed into the confines of the inner room,
was left at the mercy of shade and "shadow"[1]
diseases. Only on the arrival of the woman
physician, side by side with the evangelistic
worker, did hope spring up. As a result of
the work of the Methodist lady physicians and
nurses, Drs. Cutler and Ernsburger and Misses
Edmunds and Morrison, do we find not only
grateful patients, who have been cured and
taught, but skilful graduates, who recently
gave an exhibition of the duties of the trained
nurse before a gathering of the consular body,
Japanese officers, and army surgeons.

A large hospital has just been built inside **Hospital for Women**
of the East Gate of Seoul, that will care for
hundreds and thousands of needy women.
Women's medical work is one of the great
factors in the spread of the gospel.

A theological school has recently been started **Theological Schools**
by the Presbyterians in Ping yang, and another
by the Methodists in Seoul. This marks an-

---

[1] Shadow, contrasted with light, is one of the original emblems of the negative in nature, earth in contrast to heaven, darkness to light, woman to man.

other stage of the work. In these schools are
the choice men of the land, gathered for study
at set times of the year. The course is adapted
to the stage of the work, the attainments of
the men, and the needs of the time. Under
the leadership of Dr. Jones of Seoul, and Dr.
Moffett of Ping yang, men who have read far
into the soul problems of Korea, this part of
the work becomes a strong hope for the future. In fact, the missionary's life grows into
the life of a teacher of the few rather than a
herald to the many. While this short notice
only is given of our theological schools, seeing
that they have just begun, on the wide range
of the horizon that marks the coming history
of the Church they occupy perhaps the most
important section.

Prison-lighted Lives

Still, there are other theological schools that
have played a great and important part in the
work of missions, and one of the best of all
was the old Kamok or Criminal Prison.
Filthy, cold, infected by all the germs that
flourish in the East, crawling with vermin,
associated with crime, torture, and horrible
death, and yet a *pok-dang* or house of blessing,
it has become. The old emperor in his days
of absolute power locked in this pesthouse Yi

Seung-man, Yu Song-jun, Kim In, Yi Sang-
jai, Yi Won-gung, Kim Chung-sik. He
thought that these men meant reform along
Western lines, and they did. Without trial
by judge or jury, they were shut behind
the bars; some of them wore the cangue
collar and worked in the chain-gang. Here
they suffered from cold, from ill treatment,
from the constant fear of execution, though
they had the proud blood of a long ancestry
in their veins, and a deadly desire for
revenge in the heart. They hoped for
escape, for the opportune moment, the keen
knife, for accounts squared for time and
eternity, when all unexpectedly, there came
into their company the New Testament, Bun-
yan's *Pilgrim's Progress,* and some of Moody's
tracts in Chinese. Their prison, visited regularly by the Rev. and Mrs. A. D. Bunker,
became first an inquiry room, then a house
of prayer, then a chapel for religious exercises,
then a theological hall, and when the course
was completed, God let them all out of prison
and set them to work. With their high social
standing, with their political influence, with
their superior training in Chinese, these men
have become the first Christian leaders of the

capital. The year 1909 found Yi Seung-man
in America, taking a postgraduate course at
Harvard; Yu Song-jun is a consistent Christian in the service of the government; Yi Sang-
jai, formerly Secretary of the Cabinet, and
once Secretary of Legation in Washington,
District of Columbia, is Director of Religious
work in the Seoul Young Men's Christian
Association, and Kim In is General Secretary
of the native branch of that organization,
while Yi Won-gung, one of the most noted
Confucian scholars living, is an elder in the
Seoul Presbyterian Church; and Kim Chung-
sik, once chief of police of Seoul, is now in
charge of religious work among Korean students in Tokio. Not established under either
Methodist or Presbyterian auspices, this old
unwashed Kamok prison has been one of our
best helps. When such a means as this can be
used for God's glory, it teaches one to go
slowly and prayerfully and wait to see what
he will do.

Testings

The testing quantity has entered so deeply
into all parts of the work here that it deserves
mention. Christians who have become so without a fiery trial are of no use. This would
account for the lack of influence seen in the

lives of those who have gone abroad, become Christians, and returned. As a rule they are a hindrance rather than a help. Why is this? It is explained on the ground that they have had no Kamok Prison in their Christian experience. It has been all easy sailing. They have gone to America, have met Christians, have been helped by Christians, have become Christians, have been spoken well of as Christians, have lived with Christians, all as easy for the Oriental as for the log that floats down the stream, but on return home, when the testing-day comes, and they meet no Christians in their circle, are spoken ill of, are received coldly by society, have to live in their old world with no fighting qualities to sustain them, they are carried back into heathenism like Kipling's Hindu. A Korean Christian is not made without many strokes of the hammer, much heating of the furnace, and many testings of the metal during the long hours of the day. A place like the Kamok Prison has proved a much better Christian school than the delights and hospitalities of an American or an English home.

A house of prayer for all Eastern peoples is what God apparently means to make of this

A Gateway to
China

little peninsula. By small degrees already we see that across its border are going messages and influences that are to help great China to awake from her opium sleep of ages to see and to hear God calling, and when China awakes the world is won.

SUGGESTIVE QUESTIONS ON CHAPTER VI

AIM: TO APPRECIATE THE DEVELOPMENT OF MISSIONARY WORK IN KOREA

I. *The Native Church and the Public.*

1. What are the advantages and what the disadvantages of having it dangerous to profess Christianity?

2.* If persecution is an advantage to the native Church, what substitute for it would you recommend in a time of peace?

3. If you were a missionary, would you do anything to dispel the notion that Christianity was a religion mainly for the common people?

4. How would you, as a missionary, act if Christianity became for a time very popular?

5.* What should be the attitude of the missionaries toward Korean patriotism?

II. *Missionary Methods.*

6. In view of the hardships mentioned in the chapter, what sort of training would you recommend for a prospective Korean missionary?

7. Did the missionary do the right thing to stay

at the meeting where there was a man with smallpox?

8. Why is it so important for the missionary to have a thorough command of the vernacular?

9.* If you were a missionary beginning work, what methods would you follow in order to win the confidence of the people?

10.* Why is argument of so little use in missionary work?

11. Why is it better not to begin by attacking superstition?

12. What are the relative advantages of chapel preaching and personal interviews?

13. Why has reading been so effective with Koreans?

14. If God wishes us to evangelize the world, why do you think he has put so many obstacles in our way?

15. Try to imagine what Christianity would be like in this country if we were altogether without a Christian press or literature.

16.* Give the respective arguments for investing $50,000, in a hospital, or a college, or a press, in Korea.

17. Which parts of the New Testament do you think it would be most difficult to translate into Korean, and why?

18.* If you were appointed to translate the Bible into Korean, what various kinds of preparation would you consider necessary?

19.* Arrange the things accomplished by the medical missionary in what seems to you the order of their importance.

20. In just what way can he best dispel superstition in treating a case?
21. Why are theological schools so important on the foreign field?

REFERENCES FOR FURTHER STUDY
CHAPTER VI

I. *Methods of Work.*

Gale: The Vanguard (passim).
Gifford: Every-day Life in Korea, ch. XI.
Underwood: Fifteen Years Among the Topknots,
    pp. 130-132, 234, 235.
Underwood: The Call of Korea, ch. IV.

II. *Medical Work.*

Underwood: Fifteen Years Among the Topknots,
    pp. 133-145, 305, 306.
Gifford: Every-day Life in Korea, pp. 142-144.
Gale: Korean Sketches, ch. V.

THE RESPONSE OF KOREA

The class-leader here, who is a well-to-do farmer, so arranged his farm work this year as to devote practically his whole time, without pay, to church work. The result has been an increase of about fifty per cent. There are two churches, with Christians in eight other villages. The membership, including probationers, is 135, who with 112 other attendants make a total of 247. . . . At another point we have four churches, with three prayer rooms, and Christians in some thirty villages. Persecution at one church brought with it the stoning of two helpers, and, through their fidelity, victory, and an increase of over one hundred per cent. Here we have 306 members, including probationers, and 120 other attendants, making 426 in all. . . . During the wonderful revival that shook part of Korea the past year, until not one tile remained on top of another of the three thousand year-old devil-house, the thing that caused more remarks among the missionaries than anything else was the wonderful way in which the Koreans prayed for each other and the remarkable answers to these prayers. Not only in prayers, but in works as well, are the rank and file of the Korean Christians instant in season and out. I dare say there is no land in the world where there is so much personal and unpaid—in money—hand to hand, and heart to heart, evangelistic work done as in Korea. During the revival, when strong men were in utter despair, crying out in agony under conviction of sin, most beautiful was the way others, who had gone through the struggle and come out victorious, would go to their brother, put their arm about him and lead him into the light. The wonder of this is the greater when we remember that the Korean gives little expression to personal affection. . . . Early one morning as I was going out from Chinnampo I met one of the Christians coming in. They were having a week of prayer, and as he had pledged himself not to go empty-handed he had been out to a nearby village getting his man for the night. At the time of the women's class in Ping yang women who had received new experiences of sins pardoned and fulness of peace and joy in the new birth, came to me with tears pleading that I might go or send someone to their church that all might have this new experience and live. In some cases these women themselves were the means of bringing the revival to their local church.

—*J. Z. Moore*

VII

THE RESPONSE OF KOREA

Many years of testing by the question, Pass It On
"Where did you first hear the gospel? at
church? on the street? at prayer-meeting? by
reading the Bible?" brings the characteristic
response: "No, I heard it first from Brother
Kim, or Brother Pak, or Brother Choi; he
came to my house and we read together."
From lip to lip and heart to heart it has gone
to the distant valleys on the Manchu border,
to the windings of the Tumen, to the whirling
tides, and rocks, and cross streams of the
southern archipelago, from east to west all
over the land. God will bless Korea, for if ever
a land exemplified the Christian principle of
passing it on, it is this same country.

"The Korean Christians are unceasingly Native Christians Ever Active
active. A tract is accepted, a book is bought,
a meeting is attended, an impression made, a
desire to know more aroused; then follow
regular attendance, conversion, and entrance
into the Church. But they do not stop here.
Acquaintances, friends, and relatives are

sought, importuned, and reasoned with on
righteousness, temperance, and judgment to
come. Some of the leaders are making noble
sacrifices for the spread of the Word. In the
cold of winter and in the heat of summer; in
the crowded city and at the country market;
in the library of the Confucian scholar and in
the comfortless wayside inn; in the lonely
country farmhouse and in the privacy of the
inner room, where the women are secure from
molestation, they bear glad and cheerful testimony to the power of Christ to save from sin.
They receive abuse, accept ostracism, endure
cruel mockings and even bonds and imprison-
ments, in order to obtain a good report through
faith.

A High
Standard

"From the early days of the mission there
has prevailed among the Korean converts a
very high conception of the privileges and
responsibilities of Church-membership. A
Korean Christian is always more than a mere
Church-member; he is a worker giving his
services freely and gladly to extend the knowledge of Christ among his neighbors. It has
not been an unusual thing for a pastor of a
local church to have not less than one third of
the entire membership of his church on the

streets on a Sunday afternoon engaged in house to house visitation and personal work among their unconverted neighbors."

Thus has the work gone on and on. The native Christian has proved himself a master hand at passing on the divine message. No fiery cross of ancient Scotland ever circled the hills with more persistent rapidity than the Good News has gone throughout Korea. Each has heard from a brother, from a sister, and like propagates like; oats, oats; barley, barley; never wheat, pumpkins; nor gooseberries, pomeloes. One of the matters to fear and pray over on the mission field is that a defective Christian will lead others to the faith who will be similarly defective. Still, although Korea has her share of imperfect saints, there are among them a wonderful group of single-hearted, simple-minded, earnest, faithful Christians.

The Work Extends

"The Korean not only memorizes Scripture; he puts it into practise. One day there came into one of the mission stations a sturdy Christian from the north. After the usual greetings, he was asked the purpose of his visit. His reply was: 'I have been memorizing some verses in the Bible, and have come to recite

Doers of the Word

them to you.' He lived a hundred miles away, and had walked all that distance, traveling four nights—a long stroll to recite some verses of Scripture to his pastor, but he was listened to as he recited in Korean, without a verbal error, the entire Sermon on the Mount. He was told that if he simply memorized it, it would be a feat of memory and nothing more; he must practise its teachings. His face lighted up with a smile as he promptly replied: 'That is the way I learned it. I tried to memorize it, but it wouldn't stick, so I hit on this plan. I would memorize a verse, and then find a heathen neighbor of mine and practise the verse on him. Then I found it would stick.' Imagine this humble Korean Christian in a heathen city, amid the hills of the peninsula, taking that matchless moral code and, precept by precept, putting it into practise in his life with his neighbors. Is it any wonder that the Korean Church grows?"

Ideal for the
Native Church

The ideal for the native Church toward which all missionary agencies are striving has been that of a body which shall be self-propagating and self-governing and self-supporting. A striking testimony as to the way in which the Korean Church is realizing this ideal comes

CHURCH BUILT BY KOREANS

METHODIST CHURCH, WONSAN

from the report of Dr. Sharrocks, of Syen chun, written in 1906:

"Last year in our station of Syen chun we Self-propagation had 6,507 adherents; this year there are 11,943. From whence the 5,436 conversions during the twelve months?—an average of 453 per month. Could this be the result of our small band of missionaries? Could it be from the $72 spent on local evangelists during the year? The Koreans have 15 native evangelists giving their whole time to the work and receiving their support from the native Church. The Christians themselves have pledged a certain number of days of voluntary preaching or special definite evangelistic effort, the sum of which has exceeded 8,000 days. There have been 1,164 baptisms during the year, almost one hundred per month,—an average of 22 every Sunday. Nor is that all, these one thousand one hundred and sixty-four people were Christians for over a year before they were baptized. At the end of a few months from conversion they were examined and at the expiration of twelve months more they were again examined. If the examination was good, and if the past year's history was what a Christian's ought to be, they were baptized.

The 5,436 converts of this year will be up for examination and baptism next year. In the face of these facts I think we can call the Korean Church self-propagating.

Self-government   "In our station we have 78 churches and, as I said, 11,943 Christians. These churches are scattered over an immense territory, with picked men (unsalaried) over the individual churches. The churches are made up into circuits or groups of churches, 13 in all, with 13 assistant pastors or helpers over them. These 13 helpers are beholden to four clerical missionaries, two of whom are on furlough this year, and one of the others is yet studying the language. Could one man adequately care for 78 churches with nearly 12,000 Christians? The Church in Korea comes pretty close to being self-governing.

Self-support   "One of the national characteristics of the Korean is poverty. The daily wage is from fifteen to forty cents, which would not be so bad were the living expense not at about the same figure. To 'save up' is beyond the ordinary Korean, yet look at the finances of the Church! In our station we have 56 day-schools with 1,192 pupils, receiving not one dollar of foreign money. There are 70 church buildings in our province into only two of which any foreign money has gone. There is not a native preacher or evangelist or teacher in our province on foreign salary, though three still receive a small portion of their salaries from foreign funds. The entire running expenses of our station including everything but $350 for the hospital and the missionaries' salaries, as compared with the gifts of the native Church, are as one to ten and sixty-two hundredths—in other words, for every American dollar invested in them, our Koreans have put up ten dollars and sixty-two cents. We feel that our Church can well be called self-supporting.

"From the first the Koreans were made to believe that the spread of the gospel and growth of the Church was their work rather than ours. We are here to start them and guide them in their efforts, but it is theirs to do the work. Whether a man believes or not, is his gain or loss and not ours. He is taught that his coming into the Church confers no favor upon the missionary nor enriches the kingdom, but is a decided benefit to himself. When a man is converted, we rejoice not for our sakes, but for his. In employing workmen

Appeal to Right Motives

it is the work that tells, and if a heathen is found to give better service than a Christian the latter is dismissed and the former retained. So careful have we been along these lines that no one thinks of coming into the Church for mercenary motives."

A True "Yoke-fellow"

Another testimony comes from Dr. George Heber Jones: "From the earliest years of the mission, the Koreans have been taught that the final and complete evangelization of their people rests with them, and that the purpose of the foreign missionary is to inaugurate the work and then coöperate with Korean Christians in extending it. This position has been accepted by the Korean Christians and the Korean type is that of a man who places all his posessions in the hands of the Lord for his work. A happy illustration of this occurred in our work in the north district. Dr. W. Arthur Noble led to Christ a sturdy specimen of the northern Korean. He was the first convert in his village, and his house was the first meeting-place. After awhile the village church grew too large for its quarters and put up a chapel of its own. Then there was a debt which had to be paid. There was no money with which to pay it, as the little group had

exhausted their resources. This leader, however, had one thing he could sell—his ox with
which he did his plowing. One day he led it
off to the market-place, sold it, and paid the
debt on the church. The next spring when the
missionary visited this village he inquired for
the leader and was told he was out in the field
plowing. He walked down the road to the
field, and this is what he saw: holding the
handles of the plow was the old, gray-haired
father of the family, and hitched in the traces
where the ox should have been were this Korean Christian and his brother, dragging his
plow through the fields that year themselves!
Doubtless also there was another whom mortal
eye could not see, with form like unto the Son
of God, hitched in the yoke with these humble
Korean Christians, making their burdens light
and the yoke easy that year."

The Korean is a preacher of the gospel by   **Self-denying**
a kind of spiritual instinct; he knows and does   **Giving**
this one thing only; he provides for his Church
schools without a cent from the homelands;
he writes now and publishes his own books;
he gives up tobacco and other useless expend-
iture to save for the gospel's sake; he gives
of his means a tenth or more; sometimes he

gives all he has over a bare living. Last year, to give an example, the membership of Yun-mot-kol Church, Seoul, with income not one tenth of the ordinary city church at home, gave over ten dollars gold a member, or $3,850 for 350 members.

Donation of Time

And what an example the Koreans have set the Christian Church all over the world in their donations of time for the Lord's work! Their evangelistic effort has been systematic as well as eager. Opportunity is given at meetings for Christians to pledge a specified number of days during the coming year for work among their unconverted neighbors. This is in addition to what is done on the Sabbath. Individuals have sometimes pledged several weeks during a single year. Then campaigns are mapped out, and in some cases whole regions have been systematically evangelized. These time donations are also much in evidence when church buildings are to be erected. Not only those in whose homes money is an infrequent and hasty visitor are glad to contribute their strength, but those more well-to-do, brought up to consider manual labor a thing that no gentleman would engage in, have put their hands to the saw and the shovel. It is not remarkable that such a Church should experience a wonderful revival.

It was in 1906 that the native Christians joined heart with the foreign missionaries in an earnest prayer that God in heaven would look down in mercy and give what the heart longed for, what the hungry soul needed, what the spirit craved for in its thirsty land. What did they want that they were in such unrest over? They had health, and peace, and comfortable homes. They had friends, they had every evidence of blessing. A great Church had been gathered, what was the matter with them that they were in such an agony of distress?

Longings for Revival

It was in August that Dr. Hardie of Wonsan came to Ping yang, and in telling of the work of grace that God had wrought in his own soul, he aroused more intense and deeper longing than ever. Mr. Lee writes: "He came and helped us greatly. . . . There was born of these meetings the desire that God's Spirit would take complete control of our lives, and use us mightily in his service."

Deepening of the Movement

The old walls that had heard all the devil noises, and seen the blasted hopes of eastern Asia for fifty centuries, heard now prayers

Accumulating Power

daily that knew no cessation. But it was like
praying into space, for there was no wonderful
manifestation, nor any special answer. Things
were as they had always been. The same sun
shone, the same gray earth and brown hills
mocked them, the same birds made light of it.
Why should they pray? Give it up and be
happy. Thank God for his good gifts and
blessings. Thank him for forgiveness. Thank
him for a promised home in heaven. Be
reasonable! It may in the end reach fanaticism
if we be not careful. But you may not reason
with the swell of the ocean or the tidal wave.
Some hidden power unseen lifts the mighty
weight of water, and to try to stem it with
our feeble words would be as wise as such
reasonings with these praying souls. The
months of autumn dragged by, the last of
1906. Into 1907 the year was launched, and
still daily groups gathered for prayer. From
all points of the north land, too, came Christians to the study class, seven hundred of them!
What had they come for? To study the Bible,
of course; to get hold of who Matthew was,
and John, and the rest of them; to find what
were the leading thoughts of Paul's Epistles,
and perhaps the Book of Revelation. They

had walked, some of them, a hundred miles, some more, some less, carrying their rice on the back which was to serve as board while attending. It was quite the thing this going to Ping yang to study. They would sing hymns, and hear sermons, and rejoice and be glad, and go home and tell others about it. Now they are gathered, and when the evening meetings commence the great church is filled; fifteen hundred people. Little did these country folk dream of what was before them. Had they seen all, doubtless many would have turned back, flying for their lives in fear and consternation.

For several days the ordinary meetings were **The Crisis** held, till at last came Sunday night to which all had looked forward with great hope and expectation. Dr. Baird took the service. Under his leadership they expected to win what they hoped for, but instead it was a dry tasteless meeting. All the powers of Satan seemed to be against them. "Dead?" said Keel, "Oh you never experienced anything like it, the whole place was just *whing* with nothingness. Some tried to confess, some tried to pray. It would not do, and the meeting dispersed and went home." Intensified in their

under the fearful pall of conviction. The day
of judgment had come, and squirm and dodge
as they would, there was no escape, none
whatever. It was death; die they must. At
the sound of the preacher's voice and in face
of the conscious presence of a great and awful
God, what were they to do? And yet they
could not confess; to unveil the secrets of the
past would be shame unspeakable, and social,
material, eternal ruin. They would say, "I
am undone. I am a lost man," and let it rest.
Some did try this but found no relief, more
fearful than ever were the pent-up agonies of
the soul. Name it they must and so rid the
breast forever. Keel, in this moment of inspi-
ration, was to the crowd as John the Baptist.
"Confessing their sins." Confess was the
word that he was compelled to say, and confess was the act they were compelled to do.
It was a life and death struggle, every man
with the angel on the banks of the Jabbok.
All the reasonings of the heart came in to
restrain them. "It will defile the ears of the
hearers if I confess." "It will disgrace my
family." "It will socially ruin me." "It will
hurt the Church." "I'll die, but I can't
confess."

Pastor K. C. Pang was present, and two No Escape years later, when telling the writer, said: "It was a great sign and wonder, just as though Jesus were present right there, and there was no escape. I saw some struggling to get up, then falling back in agony. Others again bounded to their feet to rid their soul of some long-covered sin. It seemed unwise that such confessions be made, but there was no help for it. We were under a mysterious and awful power, helpless—missionaries as well as natives."

A wave of prayer would then take the as- A Mother's Deed sembled multitude, and all would join at once, mingling their petitions with cries of agony. Then in a cessation this one and that one would arise, and calling for mercy tell of the burden of the soul. One, a woman, had in the Japan-China war, escaping for her life with her child on her back, found it impossible to carry so heavy a burden. She then dashed the child against a tree, killed it, and ran. She had repented, had given her heart to God, but here was this awful deed returned upon her, and out it must come.

Another had found a Japanese pocket-book Restitution of Money which contained six hundred yen ($300 gold). He did not know to whom it belonged, and no one came to claim it, so he had used the money. But now it was upon him like all the fiends of Buddha. Out it came, and restoration had to be made, while those congregated, with eyes starting out of their heads, listened.

Surrender for Punishment

Another, years before, had been, like Barabbas, a robber. All the dark deeds of that time were on him, and now, like the rending of his soul, out they came. Immediately he gave himself up to the police and was locked up in jail.

One of my best friends, an elder in the Presbyterian Church, was there. He said that the solemnity of the meetings was beyond words to describe, something terrible, and yet one was impressed by the fact that it was right and true and holy. Years before he said he had paid off a debt and received a clear receipt, but in the paying he had not met all the requirements. He had taken advantage of one of the interested parties being dead to have it settled easier for himself. Said he: "This came back on me like a whirlwind, and the awfulness of the deed was like a lost eternity. I could not escape, so in tears and

BIBLE TRAINING INSTITUTE, PING YANG

PRESBYTERIAN CHURCH, PING YANG

contrition I had to rise and tell it to my shame and resolve to make restitution. Then a peace, a strange, sweet, indescribable peace, such a feeling as the heart had never known before, seemed to possess me."

Another friend whom I had long known, who had fallen into sin, fallen after being a Christian, had covered it up and hidden it away, was there. He had resolved never to fall again, and no man would know. He loathed himself for having done so badly, and had told others that he was a miserable sinner. He attended the meetings and sat through several, his face strained and deathly, his heart within him appalled at the prospect. At last it was confess or die, and with one superhuman effort he was upon the platform before those hundreds of people. He told all. "Was there ever such a sinner as I? My God! My God! Have mercy on my soul!" For a time it seemed as though he would die. He beat the hard wooden flooring till his hands bled, he shrieked and begged for mercy. "Is this what sin is?" said the awe-stricken multitudes. "We never knew it was so awful. We had thought it a trifle, but, behold, here is what

Making Bare the
Deepest Sin

God thinks." This friend came out of the
fiery trial cleansed and purified. So was the
whole church lifted up into the third heaven
to hear words that no man might utter.

**Missionary
Rededication**

Missionaries were alike caught in the power
of it, and what a solemn rededication of life's
service to the Highest took place no outsider
will ever know.

**Unspeakable
Joy**

One of the striking services was illustrated
by Keel's being tied by a rope and held. He
represented thus the bondage and power of
sin. How he struggled to get away, but the
rope held him! At last, at last, in his agony
it gave way, and he rushed forth free.
"Hallelujah, I am free!" This was the note
of it, and so after each confession there
followed joy, great joy, joy unspeakable, joy
that the possessor could not tell about, joy
that no man ever dreamed of.

**A New
Ping yang**

This city of Ping yang used to be considered
the most hopeless part of Korea. It had been
a veritable cage of evil birds from all time.
Among spirit-worshiping, idolatrous Koreans
Ping yang was the vilest of the vile; and yet
now everywhere praying was heard, weeping,
singing. The world had gone mad over a
religion that the fathers had never heard of.

High up on the heights of the city a church bell marked, "Ring till Jesus comes," was calling attention to the business of the hour, which was to repent, get right with God, restore, live straight.

The boys in the middle school, modern-day young men, who had spent years in Western study, had filled up on politics and were ready to sacrifice anything in behalf of their nation, were hushed by this mystery. Elder Kim Chan-sung, who led in their meetings, told me that when they met there was silence as if no man were present, but that suddenly when the name of Jesus was mentioned the whole place was electrified by the spirit of conviction. One can never tell it. It is wrapped away, recorded on the sensitive register that will come forth on the great day when all accounts are settled.

Effect Among Boys

Little children were in no wise exempt. Something told them, wee tots though they were, that God had a reckoning on hand with sin. Many of them with the clearer eyesight of the child saw wonderful visions up in the heavenly places. Many wept over their little wayward ways and went and told father and mother, and asked forgiveness. Some children

Even Reaches Little Children

whose parents were unbelievers, went home and in tears begged them to come to Jesus. Helper Kim Ik-too of Sin chun, twenty-five miles from Ping yang, told of children who, when they asked their parents to give their hearts to God, were soundly beaten. "What rubbish is this you dare talk to us?" said the irate father, but it only made the children all the more earnest in their prayers. Beating would not stop them; glaring at them Oriental fashion was of no use; threatening to kill them only increased their zeal; in some cases the parents said, "Well I'll be smitten if this doesn't beat everything," put their fingers in their ears, and ran. In other cases they yielded and bowed down in a similar confession and worship.

Joyful
Intercession

For two weeks school studies were laid aside and the time given up to prayer. After all the sins, from murder to small spites and bickerings, had been confessed and put away, some sweet angel seemed to come and clothe the lads with quietness. In the ineffable purity of the wake of this storm, prayers were poured out for others. All day long was too short to pray. Formerly it had been tiresome to weather through a single prayer-meeting

MEMBERS OF BIBLE CLASS, FOUR WALKED 100 MILES TO ATTEND

UPPER CLASS, PING YANG THEOLOGICAL SCHOOL, PING YANG

hour, now meals were forgotten in the joy of intercession.

The range of the influence too was one of the marvels. Old conservative Koreans who had drunk deep of Confucius and had worshiped every conceivable god, whose pride of spirit made them unapproachable, were among the broken-hearted and the contrite. Women who had been victims of every vile circumstance of life, were given heavenly vision and purity. Little children prayed the night through and saw wonders that Joel said some children were to see. Western missionaries, trained in other lands and formed of other human flesh, were likewise brought low down. They do not say much about it to-day and advertise it not at all, but they do emphatically declare that it was one of God's great wonders, and that they expect to see nothing like it till the gates of paradise unfold and God himself is with us.

Japanese too were blessed. Mr. Murata, a Methodist pastor, who had seen actual hostilities in the late war, and had been decorated for distinguished service, was present, and in the abundant blessing said in his broken English, "Oh tanks, tanks, tanks! Had I not

Japanese Testimony—The City Canvassed

come, I had not known to be fulfilled with the Spirit." As one result, the whole city of 50,000 inhabitants was mapped out and every man heard the gospel from some earnest heart blessed to overflowing.

To all parts of the land word had gone, and here and there similar manifestations occurred. From the old city of Seoul went a delegation asking for Keel; that he should come and speak to them, dear blind Keel! Led through the streets of the capital, he takes command of the meetings. What a thrill of influence accompanied, what deep and lasting results followed, even as conservative a man as Dr. W. D. Reynolds whole-heartedly acknowledges. Mr. Yi Chang-jik, for fifteen years a Bible translator and Christian writer, followed these meetings with the keenest of interest. He had no use for hysteria. "Besides," said he, "Koreans are inclined to make a habit of such extravagances and to think them real." But Yi was brought to his knees in a single meeting, and then went to Keel saying, "Please pray for me." "I watched Keel," said he, "was in the room with him. He seemed to pray all night, pray all night and then speak three or four times a day, led here and there

by the hand, and never seemed to be tired.
His words were like a prophet's risen from the
dead, none could withstand them." In Seoul
also many repented and flocked to the meetings. To this day permanent and lasting
results go on and on.

Wider than Korea have the influences
extended. Sometimes we say, "Would that
some colossal force might lift China; would
that God might get under China and break her
up forever;" with her submerged millions,
alive and not alive, human and yet hardly
human, sane and yet insane, filled with all of
hell and almost none of heaven, dense as
armor-plate in the matter of conscience and
soul. What can save China? Can poor
humbled Korea count for anything in the lift-
ing of China's millions? In Mukden, Manchuria, they had heard of great revivals in the
land of Korea. Two elders would come and
see. But they came too late, and the meetings
were over. Ping yang was quiet, there were
no special gatherings, and the old world had
returned. Why had they come so late?
What made their mission impossible was the
fact that they could not speak Korean, and no
one in Ping yang could speak Chinese. But

Chinese Seeking
Light

they had come Chinese-like all out of sense
and season. We are told that they called first
on some non-christian Chinese merchant and
asked if there were any *Yesoo Chow* (Christians) in Ping yang. "Plenty," said the merchant. "Are they good?" "Yes can do," was
the reply. "How do you know? You are
not a Christian." "Know? My belong
merchant I savez. Korean man no good pay.
One man very bad catchee much merchandise
no pay, never will pay, never can pay.
Afterwards same man came all makee pay up.
My velly glad. I say, 'Why you pay now?
You no pay before.' Korean man say, 'Now
I belong Christian, not Christian before, now
I pay.' Yesoo Chow velly good."

Prayer Together   They met with Keel and others of the
leaders and they walked in silence together
through the city. They prayed, the Chinese
in their unintelligible monosyllables, and the
Koreans in their world-forgotten language of
antiquity. Back to Mukden they went. Mr.
Goforth, too, came at about the same time.

*Prof. Brown on
the Manchurian
Revival*   As to the results I will let Prof. J. Macmillan
Brown tell from a special article recently
written. Prof. Brown is a hard-headed
Scotchman, a graduate of Oxford, professor

of English Literature for years, and a non-christian. He says: "The Manchurian revival began in Liaoyang on the return of two elders from Korea, bringing news of the spread of religion in that country. They and Mr. Goforth, a Canadian missionary from Ho-nan, who had also just visited Korea, gave an account of the movement to the church at Liaoyang. And at once similar phenomena took place. They came to Mukden and the excitement began there in the same way. It was here that Mr. Webster's personal observation of the movement began. He tells of the crowded church, and the sudden emotional infection that seized it without apparent cause; for the evangelist gave his story in a quiet tone and unimpassioned way. Twice a day the crowd came through the miry streets (and there is nothing to surpass the mire and ruts of Mukden) and the bitterly cold winter air to listen to the story and the appeal. Men and women broke into fervent prayer who had never uttered a prayer in public before. Strong men broke into sobs and threw themselves on their faces and wept. Others made wild confession of the sins of their former life. All vied with each other in generous gifts to the cause of evangelism, and in restitution to those whom they had wronged. They offered land, houses, a tenth or more of their incomes or salaries. Some offered gifts in kind; like a Chinese, who said he had received a great blessing, and had nothing to offer by way of expressing his gratitude 'except a black calf with a white stripe' which he offered. Then volunteers came forward and went out to the villages all over the province to tell of the strange thing that had occurred, and to stir like enthusiasm.

Words of
Missionaries

"One or two extracts from the letters of the missionaries will describe it better than anything second-hand. 'Even outsiders have been drawn into the tempest of confession and prayer, and in some cases great fear has fallen on the neighborhood. One man who had been associated with highway robbers, and had been submitted to torture during six months to extort a confession from him, but in vain, came forward at these meetings and confessed his sins and writhed in agony on the floor for a long time.' Dr. Phillips of Newchwang writes that he had 'a strong temperamental prejudice against revival hysteria in all its forms,' yet he describes a meeting he attended as something beyond his experience and outside the range of mere hysteria: 'The very air was electric, and above the sobbing in strained choking tones men began to make confession. Words of mine will fail to describe the awe, and terror, and pity of these confessions, mostly of trivial offenses yet leading to bitter remorse; it was the agony of the penitent, his groans and cries, and voice shaken with sobs; it was the sight of men forced to their feet and impelled to lay bare their hearts that moved one.'

" 'At Fakumen, seventy miles to the north-west of Mukden, it was the same storm of prayer, confession, and agonized weeping, and boundless generosity. Two men confessed each to murder and looting during the Boxer year. Many fell in a trance on the floor. Such crowds inside and outside the church had never been thought possible before at Fakumen.' 'At Hailuncheng, recently colonized, after a period of indifference the whole audience fell on their faces, loudly crying for mercy.' " *Interest at Fakumen and Hailuncheng*

Prof. Brown, in the article previously re-ferred to, goes on to say: "It would be a remarkable movement in any part of the *An Unprecedented Movement* world; it is unprecedented and striking in China."

But One
Explanation

Thus from the sorrows of this old land, and through the instrumentality of many praying Christians, there has gone forth this light that is flashing on and on through the palpable darknesses of China. Who but the Spirit of God was back of it? Who but he could so unveil the mysteries of the soul? Who make these sordid, cankered races appreciative of the pure and beautiful?

No Defense
Needed

There are no criticisms to offer. Why was it thus and thus? Why such confessions? Why not more order? Where were the Methodist Discipline and the Presbyterian Rules for Worship? These are all vain and useless questions. The whole revival was after the order of persistent prayer; it was according to the needs of the time and place; it was of God, and so let all the earth be silent.

Keel's
Conclusion

The writer was far away in America when the revival took place. Keel wrote him a letter on the 25th day of the first Moon, right in the whirl of it, and among other things he said: "If God had not manifested thus his Spirit, the Church of Korea would have been great only in appearance, but Satan would have ruled, and I fear few would have been saved. No power can tell of the blessing, nor can I write with pen all that God has done. My prayer is that the Spirit may be poured out on you as he has been manifested here."

In all the wonders of the ages, that the ancient walls of Ping yang have enclosed and looked down upon—wonders that have included the splendors of the Tangs, the Hans, the Mings; wonders that are known nowhere but in the tinted and highly-colored East— the strangest, the most inexplicable, the most awe-inspiring wonder has been the turning of these long-lost races back to God.

Ping yang's Supreme Wonder

SUGGESTIVE QUESTIONS ON CHAPTER VII

AIM: TO APPRECIATE THE RESPONSE WHICH THE KOREANS ARE MAKING TO THE GOSPEL

I. *Self-propagation by the Native Church.*

   1. Is it not the main business of the missionary to preach the gospel?

   2. Has he any right to surrender this work to others?

   3.* What advantages has the missionary as an evangelist over the native Korean?

   4.* What advantages has the native Korean over the missionary?

5. Do you think that the Roman Catholic Church would succeed in Anglo-Saxon countries, if it never employed any but Italian priests?

6. Criticise this policy, and apply your criticism to the work of missionaries in Korea.

7. If you were a missionary, how would you try to secure the coöperation of your converts in evangelistic work?

8. When you had succeeded, what work would you reserve for yourself?

9.* How would you guard against the spread of false and superficial views by recent converts?

10. To what extent do you think the Korean principles of self-propagation could be profitably applied in this country?

II. *Self-government by the Native Church.*

11. What are the dangers in placing so much responsibility for self-government upon the native Church?

12. What are the advantages of native self-government?

13.* Sketch what you would consider an ideal plan for the government of a native Church.

14. What effect would the patriarchal ideas of the Koreans have upon self-government?

15.* How would you seek to develop initiative among the native leaders?

16. How would you secure coöperation and self-government among the laity?

III. *Self-support by the Native Church.*

17.* What are the arguments for a free use of foreign money in building up the native Church?

18.* What are the arguments for requiring the native Church to meet all its own expenses?

19. What things can the Church at home wisely provide for the Korean Christians?

20. Has a field so responsive as Korea any right to ask for more missionaries?

21. Apply to yourself personally and to your locality the lessons to be learned from the Korean Christians.

REFERENCES FOR FURTHER STUDY.
CHAPTER VII

I. *Korean Response.*

Bishop: Korea and Her Neighbors, pp. 346-350.
Underwood: Fifteen Years Among the Topknots, pp. 185, 189, 193-196, 310-318.
Gifford: Every-day Life in Korea, pp. 160-162, 225-228.

II. *Self-support.*

Gifford: Every-day Life in Korea, ch. XIV.
Underwood: The Call of Korea, pp. 145, 146.
Underwood: Fifteen Years Among the Topknots, pp. 132, 133, 145, 146.

III. *Obstacles to Receiving Christianity.*

Gifford: Every-day Life in Korea, pp. 158-160, 163-169.

IV. *The Revival.*

Underwood: Fifteen Years Among the Topknots, ch. XIX.

GROWTH, PRESENT CONDITIONS, AND OUTLOOK

Are Koreans capable of high attainment? This question was asked the writer in April, 1903, by Captain Crown, commander of the Russian gunboat *Mandjure*. I replied, "We are experimenting; not convinced as yet." He went on to say, "I have never been in Korea, but know something of Koreans. It came about in this way: In 1870 my father was governor of Eastern Siberia, and on a journey in the winter from Vladivostok to Nikolaievsk, we passed many Koreans who had come north over the border. One evening, on the side of the roadway, we saw some blankets heaped up together and wrapped about something. My mother had one of the Cossack guards dismount and find out. The quilts covered two little Korean girls, who were almost perished. They were taken into the sled, wrapped up warm, and became members of our family. A month later we were called to St. Petersburg, and they went too. They grew up excellent students, both, one remarkably so, as she far outdid me in mathematics and English. After graduation, one went out to Vladivostok as a missionary of the Greek Church to her own people and there died; the other is to-day governess in the home of the Grand Duke of Constantine and has care of his little daughter. She rides out in her fine carriage and has her letters handed to her on a silver tray and is one of the most cultured ladies I know."

—*James S. Gale*

We are pressed on every side by men and women who want us to teach them about Christ. We have a hundred more invitations than we can accept. Last fall some Koreans came in to see me and asked me if I could come out to their village at once and teach them. When I told them that I could not go they pulled out some bank notes and asked me if I would go if I were paid. They were in earnest. So it is all over this great district. I could keep six missionaries busy all the time, and then have work for more. Korea can be won for Christ, and in this generation. If the Church will give us what we ask for now and strongly reinforce our work in the next ten years, this old heathen nation will line up with the other Christian nations of the world. It can be made the first-fruits of the Church in the Orient. It must be done quickly. Our opportunity is rapidly passing away. New forces are at work which are making it more difficult for us to work. What is done must be done now.

—*E. M. Cable*

VIII

GROWTH, PRESENT CONDITIONS, AND OUTLOOK

Each new year's statistics from Korea Remarkable Progress seems more remarkable than the last. The first converts were baptized in the summer of 1886. By 1890 the number of converts connected with all missions was somewhat over 100. As compared with many other fields, this is a rapid growth. Dr. Beach's *Geography and Atlas of Protestant Missions* gives the figures at the end of the year 1900 as follows: "All Protestant missionaries including wives, 141; stations, 26; outstations, 354; communicants, 8,288. The latest statistics available read: missionaries, 248; stations, 37; outstations, 1,149; communicants, 50,089; adherents, 111,379. Some striking details of growth in the number of communicants in two denominations are as follows:

Methodist Episcopal Church

1902	5,855
1905	7,796
1908	24,246

Presbyterian Church in the U. S. A.

1902	6,395
1905	9,756
1908	19,654

The following reports are characteristic:

"More new churches, more new communicants, and more contributions than ever before in one year."

"Ping yang records 2,206 communicants for 1908, as compared with 1,106 for the preceding year."

"Syen chun reports 1,388 baptisms and 2,045 additions to the catechumens during the past year."

"Already the country is waking up and a new era is dawning. The fullest possible religious liberty is enjoyed and the opportunity which opens before the Church is of a marvelous character. The people at large are turning to the Church in multitudes. They are convinced that Christianity offers the only salvation for them, and that through its ethical and spiritual power alone they will be able to develop a manhood equal to the new opportunities which open before them. On the other hand, the Church itself is alive as never before;

METHODIST CHURCH, SEOUL.

and the native Christian leaders are planning for nothing less than the evangelization of the nation. The new Korea will be a Christian Korea and that within a comparatively short period of time. Churches are multiplying in all directions. It is not possible for a foreign missionary to keep in personal touch with the multiplied groups which spring up everywhere. Evangelistically, the opportunity of the Asiatic continent of the present day is to be found in Korea. No other field compares with this in the urgency and the promise of its condition. This is the strategic people and the present is the strategic time in this land. Ten millions of souls await help and instruction which the Christian Church can give.

"The growth of the Church in Korea furnishes a bright promise of the speedy evangelization of this people. The first converts under the Methodist Episcopal Church were reported in 1888 and numbered thirty-eight. In 1907 the total following of the Church was 39,613—an increase over the beginning of over a thousandfold. An examination of the statistics of the mission will show that the ratio of increase has practically been maintained from the beginning, and all signs indi-

Methodist Episcopal Church Growth

cate that this increase may continue for an indefinite time. It is easy to work out marvelous results with figures in connection with any enterprise, but when one contemplates the numerical growth of the Church in the Korean field the result must be a great strengthening of the faith of the Church in the complete success of its mission to the world. In Korea we have a field in which there is promise of the rapid evangelization of the entire nation, and whose very condition constitutes an imperative call to the Church to concentrate her effort on the great work of giving a people so ready for it the gospel of Christ. The results reported in Korea have been achieved in the midst of a poverty of men and resources which might well have daunted the best workers. The Korean mission has had fourteen men, thirteen wives, and thirteen Woman's Foreign Missionary Society workers, or a total of forty. We are confident that if the Church had given Korea five times the number of missionaries the field now possesses, the results in converts would have been many times what they are. There has been in Korea only one native worker for each 660 of the Church-membership, and only one missionary (man) for each

CHRISTIAN MEN GATHERED FOR TWO WEEKS' BIBLE STUDY

1,630 Church-members. Taking the past three years into consideration, the average rate of increase in Korea has been over 33 per cent. If this rate of increase is maintained for a period of ten years, there will be in the care of our mission in Korea a total Church-membership of over 400,000."

"At a meeting of our pastors and preachers in Seoul the question was asked them as to the extent of our work. The answer was that our present enrolment of forty-five thousand must be multiplied by ten to express the number who to-day stand just outside the threshold of our Church in Korea, ready to accept the Christian faith if we only give them the chance. It is a matter of men and money *now*. The present conditions will not abide permanently in Korea. To-day Christianity is the national enthusiasm of the Korean people. Surely, half a million souls are worth a supreme effort upon our part as servants of the Christ who died upon the cross—yea, and arose and ascended for us. Are not all these things providentially related? Is not this the finger of God?"

A notable feature of the work in Korea has been the Bible training classes. The follow-

Number Now Accessible

Bible Training Classes

ing extracts from a Board report will give
some idea of their present growth:

Class Methods
of Work

"The conduct of the annual Bible class for
men was a matter for grave concern, with only
one clergyman in the station and probably over
600 to be instructed. As a consequence we
were obliged to depend more largely than ever
on the native helpers and colporteurs. The
class was attended by over 500 from a distance, and among them was a large proportion from the most outlying regions of our
work. A number came 100 miles to attend."
"The way the Christians lay aside their work
and attend these classes for Bible study is a
constant wonder and delight. Those who
study bear their own expenses; and in the city
we assess each student a small amount to pay
the running expenses of the class.

Impressive
Results

"The winter class in the city was attended
by about 900 men from all parts of the province. While there was none of that terrible
conviction and confession of sin of the year
before, it was a time of deep consecration to
the Master's service. The after effects were
very evident in the country churches. Altogether there have been held 151 classes for
men in the country churches, attended by

6,575 persons. The three city classes were
attended by about 1,500 persons." "The midwinter Bible class for men in February had
an attendance of 800, a gain of 300 over last
year. The men came from all the churches
and remained for instruction ten days. After
effects appeared in a series of small classes
held by the Koreans themselves at various
places. The yearly growth of this midwinter
class, the interest of the students, and their
zealous though laborious efforts at note-tak-
ing attest the value that the Koreans themselves set upon them."

"The largest class ever held in Korea was **Large Classes**
held in February in the Syen chun church.
Five Bible study classes for men were con-
ducted by the men of the station during the
year, enrolling over 2,500. The classes for
women have been especially well attended.
The two classes held in Syen chun enrolled
660. Miss Samuels held sixteen classes during the year, enrolling 2,458 women."

An illustration of another type of Bible **Native Workers'**
classes, organized by native workers and held **Plan**
in the villages for all members of the
Churches, has been given by the Rev. J. Z.
Moore.

"At the close of our conference in December, I had intended to get the leaders together and make out a plan for a week of Bible study and revival services at each church on my circuits. But as with many of 'the best laid plans of mice and men' a broken arm unexpectedly brought this to an end. On the closing day of the conference, between the pains in my arm, I was wondering how we could get along without the Bible classes, and why I had been put out of service just at the time of greatest opportunity. While I was yet thinking, one of the native preachers came in bringing a paper. Knowing that I could not take charge of it, the native preacher and Church officers in attendance at the conference had met together and made out a plan whereby each of the twenty-six churches would have a week of Bible study and revival services under the leadership of two tried and true men. They had sent me a copy of the plan that I might know where each man would be and follow him with my prayers.

"I awaited with expectation the results of these classes. Soon reports began to come in that they were having good times in the country, but I had no definite report till these

same native preachers and many of the Church
officers gathered in January for our theological class. I soon had them all together
for an afternoon tea and report of the classes.
Every class, with the exception of one, had
been held as scheduled, and every man had
gone to the place appointed, with the exception of two, who had exchanged places. Each
man, it should be noted, went from his home
church to another place for this work, and the
local churches bore all expenses of heat, light,
and evangelists' board. The attendance was
from 25 at the smallest church to over 80 at
the largest. In all, over 1,000, one third of
whom were women, attended the regular Bible
classes in the daytime; and the revival services
at night were attended at many places by all
who could crowd into the churches. The real
inner results cannot be told, but can be seen
all over the work. Though many of the
teachers were all too deficient in Bible knowledge, yet at each class God had 'much new
light to break forth from his holy Word,' and
at several places the revival services were just
as marked in sorrow for the burden of sin
and joy for pardon and forgiveness found, as
those of last year. Most of all, the leaders of

these meetings, many of whom had never attempted anything of the kind before, were
blessed in their own spiritual lives and built
up in the faith, learning for the first time, as
some one said at our afternoon meeting, that
'it is more blessed to give than to receive,'
and that one does not really get the gospel
until he gives to others what he has received.

Subscriptions of Time

"The greatest result of these Bible classes
and revival services in the direct and immediate extension of the kingdom is found in
what the natives call *Nal Yunbo*. On the last
day of the meetings, in the public service they
prepare a subscription paper, and each man
and woman according to his own heart, instead of giving money, gives so many days to
house to house and village to village preaching. Last year at just a few churches this
was done, but this year every church reported
on Nal Yunbo. This preaching was not only
all without pay, but some would be at personal
expense as well as time lost from their work.
Yet at one church they gave altogether over
one thousand days and at Chinnampo one
woman pledged six months of the year to
preaching. I cannot tell anything of the whole
results, but a few features from reports will

give you at least a faint idea of the workings of this unique plan.

One man said, as his house was by the side of the road, he preached to all who passed and most of them received the word gladly. Another man during three weeks preached definitely from house to house to two hundred people, fifty of whom believed. At one church fifty women were gathered in as a result of this preaching (for the women went from house to house as well as the men), and they now have started a night school, as they want to learn to read the Bible and have no time to study in the daytime. In all, new work has sprung up in over forty towns as a result of this preaching. *Fruitful Forms of Effort*

Those who justly lament the denominational differences of Christian workers on the foreign field can at least comfort themselves with the thought that things are not so bad as they are at home. There is in general closer fellowship between missionaries of different boards on the foreign field than between pastors of different denominations in this country. Korea has been especially favored in the cordiality of the relations that have always existed between the various bodies of missionaries working there. *Comity*

The translation of the Bible, a union hymnal, union magazines, both in Korean and English, and Sunday-school helps are all under inter-denominational auspices. The collegiate and academy work at Ping yang is under the joint control of the Northern Methodists and Northern Presbyterians. The converts of the Northern, Southern, Canadian, and Australian Presbyterians are united in a single Church with a single presbytery. There is a general council in which all the workers except those of the Society for the Propagation of the Gospel in Foreign Parts are represented. There has been an assignment of fields of work by mutual agreement in order to prevent overlapping, and in some cases an interchange of fields that had been already entered. This adjustment is not yet complete, but is proceeding in a fraternal spirit. Finally there has been discussed the establishment of a single Church of Christ in Korea which shall include the converts of all the Methodist and Presbyterian missions.

Young Men's
Christian
Association

The new building of the Young Men's Christian Association in Seoul is just finished. It stands in the heart of the city and the center of the land. It is, next to the Roman

MISSIONARIES AND NATIVE WORKERS

YOUNG MEN'S CHRISTIAN ASSOCIATION BUILDING, SEOUL

Catholic Cathedral, and excepting the New
Palace, the most prominent building in the
capital.   At the opening exercises there were
present representatives from China and Japan,
and on the closing day Prince Ito came and
made a speech.   The Korean Chairman, the
Hon. T. H. Yun, at the closing exercises made
an appeal to his own people to help this work.
He said: "I'll back my appeal by giving 500
yen ($250).   The Prime Minister present
gave 500 yen as well.   "This is for Koreans,"
said Mr. Yun, "and not for the foreign ladies
and gentlemen present."   A good-hearted
Christian druggist, Yi Min-sang, who gives
alms here, there, and everywhere, shouted, "A
thousand yen," and they put him down.   In
ten minutes subscriptions amounting to 6,700
yen were received, and Prince Ito expressed
his pleasure at the interest manifested.
Through the Young Men's Christian Association gateway are coming hundreds of
hungry youth for help on life's pathway.
"Teach us, tell us, guide us, show us, lead us."

Few if any mission fields in the world make
so deep an impression upon travelers as does
Korea.   About a decade ago, Mrs. Isabella
Bird Bishop wrote to America: "The Ping

Statement of
Mrs. Bishop

yang work which I saw last winter and which is still going on in much the same way is the most impressive mission work I have seen in any part of the world. It shows that the Spirit of God still moves on the earth, and that the old truths of sin and judgment to come, of the divine justice and love, of the atonement and of the necessity for holiness, have the same power as in the Apostolic days to transform the lives of men. What I saw and heard has greatly strengthened my own faith. Now a door is opened wide in Korea, how wide only those can know who are on the spot. Very many are prepared to renounce devil worship and to worship the true God, if only they are taught how, and large numbers more who have heard and received the gospel are earnestly craving to be instructed in its rules of holy living. I dread indescribably that unless many men and women experienced in winning souls are sent speedily, the door which the Church declines to enter will close again."

Spiritual Effects

A missionary writes: "We did not come to the foreign field expecting to have our own spiritual lives revived, but this is exactly what happened. The atmosphere here seems like

Northfield. Everywhere people are praying. Every Sabbath sees a congregation of about 1,000 men, women, and children gathered in the church here."

A recent graduate of Vassar, whose personal attitude toward missions was critical, wrote home to her mother from Ping yang, during the latter part of 1907, as follows: "The attitude of some authors and of many travelers toward the Koreans is simply ridiculous. They are in some respects the most remarkable people I have ever seen. It is as though they had been asleep in a deadening stupor; the result of being ground under the heel of a thoroughly corrupt and oppressive government. Christianity has come to them in the time of their greatest need, and is fulfilling that need marvelously. You know how critical my attitude is, you know that I do not stand firm for mission work in a sweeping, general way. However agnostic my attitude, I have nothing whatever to say but that the missions are saving the national life of this people, in giving them through Christianity a life that they could have in no other way.

"There is absolutely no room for argument against missions in Korea. The lives of the

A Convinced
Witness

No Room for
Argument

people are too obviously changed from hopelessness to vivid righteousness to admit of any exception. Whenever the incessant wrangling and quarreling that goes on within the dark, tiny walls of a mud house cease the neighbors will say, 'Why, so and so must have become Christians, they're so quiet.' The difference in the cleanliness of the houses is apparent to me, and even in four days I learned to pick out a Christian woman by the expression of her face. . . . You will be astonished at my utterances, but it is the inevitable result of an open-minded view of Korean conditions. The Korean is, as a result of natural temperament and a deadening government, a singularly passive, childlike man, with little ambition, no incentive, because every cent of money made was inevitably squeezed out of him by the *Yang ban* (officers-noble), and yet with brilliant intellectual capacity. He is far more of a scholar and far less a man of action than the Japanese; he has far more stability and a far more real sense of honor than the Japanese. Of one thing I am certain—of two things: that the Young Men's Christian Association is one of the strongest powers for righteous progress, that is, real progress, in Japan (and I expect to be able to say the entire East), and that Christianity is the force for good and for enlightenment in Korea, in spite of all that may be said concerning Japanese reform, governmental, educational, and social."

The Present

Buried for ages under these dragon hills, unable to lift the million pounds of pressure that has held them down, calling for help and no voice to answer, separated from light and life and hope by ten thousand miles of impassable sea and land, these young men and women have lived and died, tortured by ignorance and superstition, victims of fate, the evil eye, the Eight Characters, the Seven Stars, the wind gods, the hill devils, and all other ill spirits let loose, with no one to tell them whence they came, whither, or how, till at last in this day of revolution the load is to be lifted, and all men will be free. Even while Japan rules, and outwardly they are brought under suzerainty, inwardly the Koreans hear the note of freedom.

Thus Far the Work Only Begun

But all accomplished thus far has touched but the outskirts of the nation. It would take long pages to tell of the deliverance yet to be wrought. The thirsty land longs for leaders,

young men and young women, who will guide
and conduct along the way of intellect and
spirit, till they arrive at a place that will meet
the demands of the soul. The nation was once
a vast prison, but is now being metamorphosed
into a school where thousands of pupils are on
hand. Each has brought his little note-book
and pencil; each has learned all within hail,
to make sure of entrance. They wait, wait,
for the teacher to come. To some he has
come, and thither crowd the students, but for
the multiplying majorities there is no teacher
as yet. Western knowledge, Western religion,
the secret of the West, is what the East is
calling for. "Woe betide us, if you give it
not," echoes the eternal voice of all the ages.
Give it we must, and if you give it not some
one more highly favored will step in and
give it, but not for you. The discovery
of an unoccupied continent by Columbus was
not as great as this opening of territory on the
continent of Asia which has taken place and
is now going on in your day. Who are to be
the colonists to make the New Englands and
Virginias in this region of the intellect and
soul? You my reader, for you are here to
make your best impression on the world in

the short space of time allotted. God grant
that you make it on Asia; it is the greatest
field open and Korea is one of the keys thereto.
She is in touch with both Japan and China.
She leads Japan's life and she thinks China's
thoughts. She writes and reads a language
known to both.

Another cause that leads her into this wider
way of service is the fact that Korea's old
narrow partitions are broken down, and home
is anywhere, wide as the horizon. But the
political situation is such that she cannot go
abroad, only to China and Japan. Other
doors are closed and she is not allowed free
exit. This too is a part of the great plan, and
contributes to the end in view.

Providential Lines of Destiny

Two weeks ago the writer heard for the
first time in twenty years' experience the
sound of a Chinese voice from the pulpit of
his church. Mr. S. K. Tsao, of Shanghai,
addressing a thousand Koreans or more said:
"My heart rejoices when I see the work of
God in this land. A great field lies before you,
not only in your own country but in China.
I expect the day to come when you will send
missionaries to my land and help evangelize
it." It was a Macedonian call of the present

A Voice from China

day. The whole East is calling, and if your heart be but turned by prayer and earnest inquiry into God's Word for his thoughts and plans, you will catch the vibrations that quiver through the ether more persistently than Marconi's wireless signals: "C,O,M,E; H,E,L,P; U,S."

Vision of The East

Thou, reader, come with me till I show thee the unevangelized lands, the lands without teachers, and in the showing thou wilt see the Far East; and it will stretch away, and away, and still away, wider than the limit of thy mind to measure; and it will be peopled with millions and millions. Counting would never do it, for thou couldst never even think them all, so many and so many.

The Cry of Its Needs

What are they doing in this world? Unconsciously they grope round at this and that, tramping the treadmills of the ages, following worn ruts cut in the rocks and crumbling granite, mumbling unintelligible prayers, swearing worn-out oaths, dying in the old fearsome way, with tears and wailings and agony, being buried; on, and on, and on, millions upon millions; no churches, no hospitals, no newspapers, no schools, no books, no liberty of thought, no explanation of life,

A GROUP OF KOREAN LEADERS
DELEGATES TO WORLD'S CHRISTIAN STUDENT FEDERATION, TOKYO

no solution to the terrors of nature about them; no confidence in the neighboring states just over the way; no message from the underworld as to whether it is peopled with half beasts or only devils; in terror as to the acts of sun, moon, and stars; scared by the sea with its water-dragons and hungry beasts; in fear of the hills full of disembodied spirits; cut off from hope for spirit, soul, and body. Gaze thou on them and think and ponder well, hadst thou been born there, thou too wouldst have had the vacant eye, the soul wild with weeds, the mind shrunk, hopeless; thou too wouldst be foul of body, begrimed with dirt; thou too wouldst have had the little hovel in which to huddle; thou too wouldst have crossed life's stage a poor benighted heathen, to be laughed at, and kicked, and cuffed, and spat on by the world that thinks it sees; and in the end thy body might be left unburied till it became a terror to all living creatures.

Hadst thou two souls and one so lost as this, how that twin soul of thine would rush to earth's most distant boundary to rescue and save the soul of thine that was lost. But equally precious to any half soul of thine are these multitudes to whom all the gateways of

Soul Service and Coming Glory

the world have opened; toward whom mighty steamers plow the oceans; across whose line of vision go long lines of railway trains; into the very citadel of whose ignorance now clicks the telegraph; each of them signs and signals that God is calling thee, thou reader. This twin brother of thine is in prison; leave thou thyself and thy wishes and visit thou him; he is hungry, feed him; he is thirsty, give him drink. If thou doest this well, there will be times of suffering and sacrifice for thee and trial and self-renunciation, but thou wilt assuredly see at the close thereof the most beautiful city that has ever been founded; thou shalt be shown the way thither by the most beautiful guards of honor, and on the entrance thou shalt hear such a voice as thy ears have waited all these years to hear; and thou shalt see, in the midst of joy unspeakable and full of glory, many dearest friends of thine from the yellow lands of the East.

The East Holds the Question of Questions

The Far East is to have its innings. The time has come. For masses of humanity she leads the world, and when the president of all the earth is to be elected by popular vote, he will be a man of the yellow skin. She can do

anything; once teach her and she can do all
that we can do cheaper and easier. She is the
greatest question to-day in the whole world
of thought; fear hangs on her, untold hopes
center in her. She can hate like a branded
fiend; she can love like a little child. O thou
East, what will the end be? Truly out of thee
will come great men and good, and women
whose names will last through all ages; in
thee is infolded the solution of the world, and
the end of all its questions.

The writer was once asked, "Who is the **The Greatest Man**
greatest man you have ever met?" He pon-
dered long over the question, for he had met
kings, princes, nobility, Western and Eastern,
great rulers, writers, statesmen, inventors,
evangelists, preachers, teachers; it seemed as
though he had met everybody. Now who is
first among all these? To whom would you
give a Nobel prize as the greatest man on
earth? It would go to—not the king, nor
the millionaire, nor the inventor, nor the
preacher—but to one who was an outcast,
socially, intellectually, morally, physically, a
tramp of the streets, who came into touch with
the story of the redeemed. The sound of it,
in some way I know not how, awakened

responses in his soul. For him, could it be? He, a lost gambler, not even of average intellect, branded with all marks of sin, equal to a leper as to his physique. As he pondered and prayed and dreamed over these discovered ideals of his, he was little by little changed, the old life sloughed off, and in some miraculous way the face became gentle, benign, lighted up, beautiful; the old ways dropped off, and in place of self being all in all, others came into being, lived, and flourished. All money labored for, beyond a little rice to live by, passed on its winged way for others. Long prayers were made over a few pieces of cash, that their service might be made sure. From this castaway fragment of charcoal, that had been transformed into flashing diamond, radiated light in all directions. The poor were touched by it; ex-ministers of state were overcome by the quiet voice and the heart of love, this one, that one; proud men were brought down low when they met him; the humble were lifted up and made glad. Ko's heart enlarged so that he desired to know all about the world, its knowledge, its science. He managed addition, subtraction, multiplication; division cost him deep thought, but at last he saw through its tricks; fractions were beyond him. "Three fifths of seven eighths. That beats me," said he; "I'll give it up till I get more sense." As his horizon extended and other nations came into the circle of it, he inquired for them and put their names into his prayers. By degrees his heart widened till it took in great companies of people. Long after he had been a noted leader in Christian work, and dressed well according to his station, he came on a home of young men who were too poor to eat and too proud to do coolie work.

"Put a rack on your back," says Ko, "and you will soon make enough to pay for the winter's pickle."

"But we are ashamed," said they; "we can't face the world with a rack on the back."

"No?" said Ko, "then I'll get a rack too and go with you."

So down the Main Street of Seoul went Ko, with hat off and broad smile over his face, a rack on his back to help these young men over their fear. He made a silver dollar and gave it to the Kims for pickle. He often said, "I wonder why people are so good to me, these high nobility too, and I a castaway," and the tears would come.

Ko Chan-ik

Ko of *The Vanguard*, the same who labored and sorrowed and rejoiced and prayed with a whole world of fellow pilgrims, even the same Ko who now sleeps outside the East Gate, would get the Nobel prize for greatness. He would get it because he loved most unselfishly and patiently the greatest number of people at one and the same time; because he could hold more of humanity in his heart and plan for them, think about them, pray for them, encourage them, gladden them, and call on them, than any other mortal I have ever known. The greatest heart I ever knew—Ko Chan-ik. Thou, reader, be thou likewise.

SUGGESTIVE QUESTIONS ON CHAPTER VIII

AIM: TO APPRECIATE THE CALL OF KOREA IN TRANSITION

I. *The Future Prospects.*

  1. On the basis of the figures of 1890, 1900, and the present, what may we expect to see in Korea in 1920?
  2. What rate of future increase is indicated by the figures for 1902, 1905, and 1908?
  3. In which decade of missionary work should we expect the most rapid rate of increase, the first, second, or third?

4.* Sum up the influences that tend to increase the rate of progress in the evangelization of a non-christian land as time goes on.

5. Mention circumstances that might check this rate of increase.

6. What is the lesson to the Christian Church of these possibilities?

II. *Korea an Object-lesson to Asia.*

7.* What would be the special value to the Far East of having an entire nation in Asia accept Christianity?

8. Why is Korea more likely than any other nation to become such an object-lesson?

9. What will be the effect on the Far East if the Christianity of Korea is of only a superficial type?

10.* What things that Korea lacks do you think she needs most to fit her to serve as an object-lesson of Christianity?

11. What lines of work do you think missionaries should especially emphasize at present?

III. *Korea an Object-lesson to the World.*

12. Contrast the opportunities presented to Bible class leaders in Korea and in other lands.

13. How would it affect your own locality if such comity prevailed between Christian denominations as in Korea?

14. To what extent does the argument for a united Christian Church in Korea apply to Christianity in this country?

15.* Compare the present awakening of the Far East in its extent and scope with the Renaissance and the Reformation.

IV. *The Present Appeal.*

16.* Sum up the call of Korea to-day in view of the needs.

17.* Sum up the call of Korea to-day in view of the achievements.

18.* Sum up the call of Korea to-day in view of the opportunities.

19.* Defend the investment of $100,000 of missionary money in some form of work in Korea.

20.* Present missionary service in Korea as the most profitable investment of a life-work.

REFERENCES FOR FURTHER STUDY.
CHAPTER VIII

I. *The Outlook.*

Underwood: The Call of Korea, pp. 136-150.
Hulbert: The Passing of Korea, ch. XXXV.
Supplement with denominational literature and recent magazine articles.

APPENDIXES

APPENDICES

APPENDIX A

Division of Territory, Population, Distribution of Missionaries[1]

Province	Population	Missionaries	Responsibility for each
Chulla (North)	597,393	20	30,000
Chulla (South)	850,635	12	70,000
Chung chong (East)	491,717	7	70,000
Chung chong (West)	649,756	8	81,000
Hamkyung (North)	390,055	3	133,000
Hamkyung (South)	582,463	23	25,000
Kang wun	627,832	2	313,000
Kyung kui	869,020	82	10,000
Kyung sang (North)	1,062,991	13	81,000
Kyung sang (South)	1,270,214	16	79,000
Pyengan (North)	600,119	16	37,000
Pyengan (South)	689,017	37	18,600
Whanghai	901,099	8	112,000

[1] Issued by the Financial Adviser's Office and published in *The Christian Movement in Japan*, 1907.

STATISTICS OF PROTESTANT MISSIONS IN KOREA COMPILED

NAME OF SOCIETIES	Year included in the Report	Year of First Work in This Field	FOREIGN MISSIONARIES, INCLUDING PHYSICIANS			
			Ordained Men	Unordained Men	Missionaries' Wives	Other Missionary Women
AMERICAN SOCIETIES						
American Bible Society	1907	1882	1	..	..	..
Board of Foreign Missions of the Methodist Episcopal Church [1]	1908	1885	21	2	18	21
Board of Foreign Missions of the Presbyterian Church in U. S. A.	1908	1884	30	1	37	10
Board of Missions of the Methodist Episcopal Church, South	1907–8	1895	11	5	12	..
Executive Committee of Foreign Missions, Presbyterian Church in U. S.	1906–7	1896	9	4	9	4
Foreign Department, Y. M. C. A. of North America	1909	1901	3	..	..	..
Foreign Mission Committee, Presbyterian Church, Canada	1907	1898	6	..	4	4
Woman's Board of Foreign Missions, Methodist Episcopal Church, South	1908–9	1897	..	..	..	11
Total American Societies, 8	....	....	81	12	80	50
BRITISH SOCIETIES						
British and Foreign Bible Society	1908	1885	2	..	2	..
Foreign Mission Committee, Presbyterian Church of Australia	1908	1889	3	..	3	5
Society for the Propagation of the Gospel in Foreign Parts	1907	1896	4	3	..	3
Total British Societies, 3	....	....	9	3	5	8
Grand Total, 11 Societies	....	....	90	15	85	58

[1] Includes statistics of Woman's Foreign Missionary Society.
[2] 797 Churches entirely self-supporting.
[3] Includes higher educational schools.

DIX B

BY DIRECT CORRESPONDENCE WITH MISSION BOARDS

Native Workers	STATIONS		NATIVE CONSTITUENCY		EDUCATIONAL								MEDICAL			
Native Workers	Where Missionaries Reside	Outstations or Substations	Communicants	Adherents Not Yet Communicants	Sunday Schools	Sunday School Scholars	Day Schools	Pupils in Same	Higher Institutions	Students in Same	Industrial Schools	Students in Same	Foreign Men Physicians	Foreign Women Physicians	Hospitals or Dispensaries	Patients During Year Reported
16	··	19	24,246	19,820	167	14,417	144	4,407	5	545	..	..	4	4	4	17,007
282	7	²809	19,654	73,844	798	61,454	457	11,480	9	763	1	..	8	4	12	47,664
837	8	..	3,545	2,536	45	3,049	3	82	1	225	..	..	5	..	3	2,000
72	4	140	1,051	8,410	22	1,390	18	381	..	6	..	..	4	2	..	....
75	4	..	....	....	..	....	..	....	..	..	..	..	..	..	..	....
42	4	56	814	194	45	3,034	³17	305	..	..	..	..	1	1	1	300
10	3	..	....	....	..	....	4	150	..	..	1	20	..	..	2	....
1,334	30	1,024	49,310	104,804	1,077	83,344	643	16,805	15	1,539	2	20	22	11	22	66,971
85	..	..	385	3,219	6	500	8	200	..	..	..	..	1	..	1	....
30	2	..	394	3,356	..	....	3	31	1	32	..	..	..	..	..	....
··	5	125			..	....							..	..	..	....
115	7	125	779	6,575	6	500	11	231	1	32	..	..	1	..	1	....
1,449	37	1,149	50,089	111,379	1,083	83,844	654	17,036	16	1,571	2	20	23	11	23	66,971

APPENDIX C

BIBLIOGRAPHY

The first seven books mentioned in the list below are included in the Reference Library issued to accompany this text-book. Numbers eight to ten have been freely cited in the references at the end of the chapters. The last five are listed for the benefit of those who are interested in the present political situation.

GALE: Korean Sketches. 1898. Fleming H. Revell Co., New York. Illustrated. $1.00.

One of the most attractive books ever written on Korea. Useful for a person uninterested in missions, but who can appreciate clever writing. Some of the characterizations are very acute.

GALE: The Vanguard. 1904. Fleming H. Revell Co., New York. Illustrated. $1.50, net.

Perhaps the most successful missionary novel yet written. The atmosphere and phases of missionary life are hit off in most picturesque style. A splendid book to interest the indifferent.

NOBLE: Ewa, A Tale of Korea. 1906. Eaton & Mains, New York. Illustrated. $1.25.

One of the most thrilling missionary stories written. The characters and incidents are historical, and the spirit and traditions of the people have been faithfully followed.

BAIRD: Daybreak in Korea. 1909. Fleming H. Revell Co., New York. Illustrated. 60 cents, net.

A tale of the power of the gospel in transforming heathen society, and especially the life of women.

UNDERWOOD: Fifteen Years Among the Top-Knots. Second Edition, 1908. American Tract Society, New York. Illustrated. $1.50.

An account of the experiences of missionary work in Korea, described in an interesting way. The second edition contains three additional chapters covering the most recent developments of Korean missions.

HULBERT: The Passing of Korea. 1906. Doubleday, Page & Co., New York. Illustrated. $3.80, net.

A reference book by one who knows the country thoroughly. Chapters on recent history are followed by general information on varied topics. The standpoint is pro-Korean and anti-Japanese.

UNDERWOOD: The Call of Korea. 1908. Fleming H. Revell Co., New York. Illustrated. 75 cents, net.

An earnest appeal for Korea, written by one of the pioneer missionaries for use as a text-book. Brief, but full of information. An appendix contains questions on the chapters and references for further study.

GIFFORD: Every-day Life in Korea. 1898. Fleming H. Revell Co., New York. Illustrated. $1.25.

A plain and interesting account of missionary life and work in Korea up to 1897. Most of the statements about Korean character and principles of missionary method will be valuable for a long time to come.

BISHOP: Korea and Her Neighbors. 1897. Fleming H. Revell Co., New York. Illustrated. $2.00.

A journal by the well-known traveler. The form of the book is somewhat diffuse, but Mrs. Bishop's style is vigorous and her judgment keen.

JONES: Korea: The Land, People and Customs. 1907. Jennings & Graham, Cincinnati. 35 cents, net.

A booklet containing much condensed information and an account of the beginnings of the Methodist work.

ALLEN: Things Korean. 1908. Fleming H. Revell Co., New York. Illustrated. $1.25, net.

Dr. Allen was the first resident Protestant missionary in Korea, and was for a long time United States minister there. He treats in rambling style various matters observed during the last twenty-five years.

McKENZIE: The Unveiled East. 1907. E. P. Dutton & Co., New York. $3.50, net.

A sketch of conditions in China, Korea, and Japan, written from the political and commercial view-point. The author criticises Japan's administration in Korea.

McKenzie: The Tragedy of Korea. 1908. E. P. Dutton & Co., New York. $2.00, net.

A severe arraignment of the Japanese methods in Korea.

Millard: The New Far East. 1906. Charles Scribner's Sons, New York. $1.50, net.

An examination into the new position of Japan and her influence upon the solution of the Far Eastern question, with special reference to the interests of America and the future of the Chinese Empire.

Millard: America and the Far Eastern Question. 1909. Moffat, Yard & Co., New York. $4.00.

Gives some chapters on Korea as a factor in the present political and commercial situation. The verdict is unfavorable to the Japanese.

Ladd: With Marquis Ito in Korea. 1908. Charles Scribner's Sons, New York. Illustrated. $2.50, net.

A Japanese apologetic, dogmatic in tone and with little sympathy for Korea. Professor Ladd was in the employ of the Japanese government during the visit he describes.

INDEX

INDEX

A

Ague, 15

Allen, Hon. H. N., M.D., 163, 175, 180; quoted, 160

American trolley-cars, 13, 14

Analects, The, 141

Ancestor worship, 69–78

Appenzeller, Dr., 163

Australian Presbyterian work, 238

Avison, Dr., 180

B

Baird, Dr., 203

Beach, Dr., 227

Berneux, Bishop, 161

Bible, 47, 79, 88, 89, 119, 120, 140; illustrated by Korean customs, 147–155; translation, 138, 175

Bible study classes, 176, 231–236

Bishop, Mrs. Isabella Bird, 69; quoted, 2, 83, 94, 239, 240

Book of Changes, the, 47

Books of History and Poetry, the, 141

Brown, Prof. J. Macmillan, quoted, 216, 219

Brown, Sir John McL., 58

Buddhism, 66, 68, 79–81

Bunker, Rev. and Mrs. A. D., 183

C

Cable, E. M., quoted, 226

Canadian Presbyterian work, 238

Canon of Changes, The, quoted, 87

Carlyle, Thomas, referred to, 52, 54

Cash, old coins formerly used, 11, 12

Chang Chih-tung, 178

Changing conditions, 22–24, 58, 59, 146, 170

Chang-yu, Prince, 9

China, but little known in 1889 to Korea, 129; her millions on the West, 135; uses a cumbersome language, 136; voice from, 245

"Chinaman, John," 40, 41

Chinese literature in Korea, 44–46

Chinese seeking light from Korea, 215

Chinnampo, 190, 236

" Chosun," 4

Christ, see *Jesus Christ*

Comity among missionaries, 237

Confucianism, 62, 72, 78, 80, 95, 106

Coolie, the, in transportation, 12; naming the Five Virtues, 96

Crisis, the final, in Korea, 38

Forward Mission Study Courses

" Anywhere, *provided it be* FORWARD.''—*David Livingstone.*

Prepared under the direction of the

MISSIONARY EDUCATION MOVEMENT

OF THE UNITED STATES AND CANADA

EDITORIAL COMMITTEE: T. H. P. Sailer, *Chairman;* A. E. Armstrong, T. B. Ray, H. B. Grose, J. E. McAfee, C. R. Watson, John W. Wood, L. B. Wolf, G. F. Sutherland, H. P. Douglass.

The forward mission study courses are an outgrowth of a conference of leaders in young people's mission work, held in New York City, December, 1901. To meet the need that was manifested at that conference for mission study text-books suitable for young people, two of the delegates, Professor Amos R. Wells, of the United Society of Christian Endeavor, and Mr. S. Earl Taylor, Chairman of the General Missionary Committee of the Epworth League, projected the Forward Mission Study Courses. These courses have been officially adopted by the Missionary Education Movement, and are now under the immediate direction of the Editorial Committee of the Movement. The books of the Movement are now being used by more than forty home and foreign mission boards and societies of the United States and Canada.

The aim is to publish a series of text-books covering the various home and foreign mission fields and written by leading authorities.

The following text-books having a sale of 900,000 have been published:

1. THE PRICE OF AFRICA. (Biographical.) By S. Earl Taylor.

2. INTO ALL THE WORLD. A general survey of missions. By Amos R. Wells.

3. PRINCELY MEN IN THE HEAVENLY KINGDOM. (Biographical.) By Harlan P. Beach.

4. SUNRISE IN THE SUNRISE KINGDOM. A study of Japan. By John H. DeForest.

5. HEROES OF THE CROSS IN AMERICA. Home Missions. (Biographical.) By Don O. Shelton.

6. DAYBREAK IN THE DARK CONTINENT. A study of Africa. By Wilson S. Naylor.

7. THE CHRISTIAN CONQUEST OF INDIA. A study of India. By James M. Thoburn.

8. ALIENS OR AMERICANS? A study of Immigration. By Howard B. Grose.

9. THE UPLIFT OF CHINA. A study of China. By Arthur H. Smith.

10. THE CHALLENGE OF THE CITY. A study of the City. By Josiah Strong.

11. THE WHY AND HOW OF FOREIGN MISSIONS. A study of the relation of the home Church to the foreign missionary enterprise. By Arthur J. Brown.

12. THE MOSLEM WORLD. A study of the Mohammedan World. By Samuel M. Zwemer.

13. THE FRONTIER. A study of the New West. By Ward Platt.

14. SOUTH AMERICA: Its Missionary Problems. A study of South America. By Thomas B. Neely.

15. THE UPWARD PATH: The Evolution of a Race. A study of the Negro. By Mary Helm.

16. KOREA IN TRANSITION. A study of Korea. By James S. Gale.

17. ADVANCE IN THE ANTILLES. A study of Cuba and Porto Rico. By Howard B. Grose.

18. THE DECISIVE HOUR OF CHRISTIAN MISSIONS. A study

of conditions throughout the non-Christian world. By John R. Mott.

19. INDIA AWAKENING. A study of present conditions in India. By Sherwood Eddy.

In addition to these courses, the following have been published especially for use among younger persons:

1. UGANDA'S WHITE MAN OF WORK. The story of Alexander Mackay of Africa. By Sophia Lyon Fahs.

2. SERVANTS OF THE KING. A series of eleven sketches of famous home and foreign missionaries. By Robert E. Speer.

3. UNDER MARCHING ORDERS. The story of Mary Porter Gamewell of China. By Ethel Daniels Hubbard.

4. WINNING THE OREGON COUNTRY. The story of Marcus Whitman and Jason Lee in the Oregon Country. By John T. Faris.

These books are published by mutual arrangement among the home and foreign mission boards, to whom all orders should be addressed. They are bound uniformly and are sold at 50 cents, in cloth, and 35 cents, in paper; postage, 8 cents extra.

Date Due

MAR 17 '50			
APR 14 '50			
APR 26 '50			
MAY 18 '55			
MAY 25 '55			
JUL 7 '55			